Dear Peter,

May God be
with You & Bless You
now & always

Katie McCloskey

The Calling

The Calling

✦

Stories and Reflections from Working with Mother Teresa and the Missionaries of Charity in Calcutta, India

Including Words of Wisdom Shared with the Author by Mother Teresa—Blessed Teresa of Calcutta

Katie McCloskey

Compiled by: Susan Johnson Skipp

iUniverse, Inc.
New York Lincoln Shanghai

The Calling
Stories and Reflections from Working with Mother Teresa and the Missionaries of Charity in Calcutta, India

iUniverse books may be ordered through booksellers or by contacting:

iUniverse
2021 Pine Lake Road, Suite 100
Lincoln, NE 68512
www.iuniverse.com
1-800-Authors (1-800-288-4677)

Because of the dynamic nature of the Internet, any Web addresses or links contained in this book may have changed since publication and may no longer be valid.

The views expressed in this work are solely those of the author and do not necessarily reflect the views of the publisher, and the publisher hereby disclaims any responsibility for them.

ISBN: 978-0-595-45649-9 (pbk)
ISBN: 978-0-595-70783-6 (cloth)
ISBN: 978-0-595-89951-7 (ebk)

Printed in the United States of America

This book is dedicated to the people of India,
especially all of the poor in Calcutta,
and to all of the Missionaries of Charity,
and in particular our Mother Teresa of blessed memory.

You have taught me so much.
You have changed my life.

Contents

Acknowledgements

All of this book and the stories would not exist if not for Susan Skipp. Susan has the patience of all the silent saints.

My little scraps of paper, my deadlines, my bad writing. Susan took it all and shaped and molded as the book began. She spent many hours volunteering her time and talents. Heartfelt thanks were her paycheck. And thanks to Raymond, her husband, for giving up his wife on a few occasions.

Thank you to Lindsey Henrard, Simone Sebalo, Noel Michaelsen, Juli Hoffman, and Jaimee Comstock-Skipp for sharing their time and talents on the pictures and design of the book cover.

Especially to all who have lived to work in Calcutta, to all of the Sisters and volunteers who have reshaped my life into a higher purpose.

I am currently working on Volume II.

Foreword

The Calling. This book will have an impact on you like no other. A good impact. Perhaps a great impact. You will want to share it with your friends, family, co-workers—everyone you know.

Why? What makes *this* book about working with Mother Teresa, the Missionaries of Charity, the people of India, and especially the poor of Calcutta unique?

The stories.

Each story speaks for itself, revealing a message much more profound than the words on the page recount. Each story touches you. Deeply. Each story becomes a part of you. The people, the places, the situations ... you can't get them out of your mind, your heart, your soul. You muse, reflect, ponder. You come back to one story, another, and another ... time and time again.

The stories make you think. They affect you. You will not be the same person.

And each story is true. Real situations. Real people.

After one of her trips to India, Mother Teresa told Katie McCloskey to share her experiences. Sister Shanta gave her a journal and told her to write about what she had seen. After reading Katie's stories, Sister Nirmala gave her blessing. This is the result.

Having worked over a dozen years and become friends with Mother Teresa and the Missionaries of Charity (MCs) in Calcutta, Katie McCloskey has captured, in a sublime fashion, the reality of life in Calcutta. Of life in India. Of Mother Teresa and the women and men who are the Missionaries of Charity. Of the "silent saints," as Katie calls them—the countless volunteers who give of themselves to help the poor in India. Of the honesty of our human condition ... weak, broken, ever in need of change, and still with the capacity for unfathomable acts of greatness.

The Calling. It's all about responding to and sharing with others God's love. True love: selfless giving at all times and in all circumstances ... to help others ... without counting the cost.

Katie worked with Mother Teresa and the Missionaries of Charity since 1993, giving her nursing skills, her heart and her very self to the MCs and the poor of Calcutta: Kalighat, the Shishu Bhavan, the Dispensary, Titagarh. She spent time with Mother, the Sisters, the Brothers, the volunteers, Calcutta, the people of India. She worked with them, lived with them, prayed with them. She came to know them and their lives, intimately. They became her dear friends. She loved them, respected them. She observed, learned, grew. She taught them; they taught her. They became a part of her family. They became a part of Katie.

These stories leave a mark on your soul ... you can't help but want to share them.

We all have a call. Like Mother Teresa and the MCs, like Katie and the volunteers.

Thank you, Katie, for putting your love into action despite your fears. Thank you for writing about these experiences. May we all have the courage to answer His call.

"Radiating Christ"

Dear Jesus, Help us to spread your fragrance everywhere we go. Flood our souls with your spirit and life. Penetrate and possess our whole being, so utterly that our lives may only be a radiance of yours. Shine through us, and be so in us, that every soul we come in contact with may feel your presence in our soul. Let them look up and see no longer us but only Jesus! Stay with us, and then we shall begin to shine as you shine so to shine as to be a light to others; the light, O Jesus, will be all from you, none of it will be ours; it will be you, shining on others through us. Let us thus praise you in the way you love best by shining on those around us. Let us preach you without preaching, not by words but by our example, by the catching force, the sympathetic influence of what we do, the evident fullness of the love our hearts bear to you. Amen.

This is the prayer we said each day at the Mother House before beginning work in Calcutta ... all of us who worked with Mother Teresa and the Missionaries of Charity. We learned very quickly that none of us could do this work relying on own strength, our own talents, or our own abilities. We would need to draw our strength from the source. Only God could give us the courage, the perseverance, and the grace we needed to serve the poorest of the poor in India—the multitudes of the sick, the suffering, the abused, the unloved, the unwanted, the babies, the young children, the elderly, the handicapped, the broken, the starving, the dying—the likes of which you have never experienced before. To love and care for each one. Each precious life.

"... help us to spread your fragrance everywhere we go ... let us preach you without preaching, not by words but by our example...."

As Mother Teresa often said, "Love is not love if it remains by itself. Love must be put into *action*."

"... by the catching force, the sympathetic influence of what we do, the evident fullness of the love our hearts bear to you."

And to do it with great joy ... a joy that comes from within.

Thank you, Sister Nirmala and all of the Missionaries of Charity for continuing in Mother's footsteps; for being joyful witnesses to God's love ... serving him through loving and caring for the poorest of the poor in India and throughout the world.

Your example is so important in a world that is now, perhaps more than ever, in need of knowing what true love really means.

God's call ... to love ... to give the gift of self. Spread the fragrance.

Introduction

"Welcome." Mother Teresa's first word to me. This woman I had admired so much from afar was welcoming me to Calcutta. Her face was lined and wrinkled, but yet so young. Her hands, the softest I've ever felt, were touching me. Those beautiful, soft hands.

I have had the very great privilege of knowing the person I admired most in this world. She is no longer alive, but she is still leaving her mark on the world. Indeed, the world is a better place because of her calling in life and her willingness to do it.

Mother Teresa mainly caught my attention because of her statement: Everyone is a child of God. It didn't matter who you were—your color, your nationality, your background, your status, your religion. Everyone was special. Everyone was created in the image and likeness of God. Everyone was created to love. And, everyone needed and deserved to be loved.

It was apparent—this love. Mother and all of the Sisters radiated a glow, a joy. To be in their presence was a bit of heaven on earth.

I met Mother Teresa for the first time in 1993—my first trip to India. I have made more than a dozen such trips to India to work with the MCs in Calcutta. It's a part of who I am.

Each day in Calcutta you live a lifetime. You experience so much—sadness, joy, smells, noise, unspeakable sights ... a sea of humanity living in the streets amidst extreme poverty, starvation, pollution, disease, abuse, death. And many miracles. One visit. You are forever changed.

Why did I write this book? It is said that in giving we receive. As Mother Teresa used to say, "Give until it hurts you." I have had the gift of giving myself and my nursing skills to the MCs over the past fourteen years. In giving, I have received more than a hundred-fold. On my third visit to Calcutta, Mother told me, "I have been sharing with you every day, now you go and share." Before leaving, Sister Shanta gave me a journal and said, "Katie, write what you have seen." With Sister Nirmala's blessing, the time has come to share the gifts that have been given to me.

We all have different callings in life. And yet, each one of us is called to love and to spread love. Mother Teresa said we should do this first with our families, then our neighbors and communities, and then with those we meet every day. Mother said: "Never let anyone come to you without leaving happier and better." Our kindness to each other, our smiles, our greetings … nothing is ever too small.

This book contains some of the many stories of experiences in Calcutta. Each person, each situation has forever created an imprint on my heart, my soul. Writers are artists, painting pictures with words. May these words give you pictures of the beauty of Mother Teresa, the sisters, the workers, the volunteers. My wish is that they leave you a happier and better person. Each person can and does make a difference.

May God's love touch you, surround you … as it did Mother Teresa.

And, whatever your call, may your love grow into action. Spread the fragrance.

Setting the Stage

LIFE BEGINS AT 40

I always knew that I wanted to be a nurse.

When I was four years old, I would take scissors and cut out pictures of nurses in magazine ads for "The Post School of Nursing." When I was nine or ten years old, I wrote to the Post School to see if I could apply. They never wrote back. But that was okay. I knew that I was going to be a nurse.

Life progressed. I began to develop a great fear of sickness and hospitals. Death, blood, and trauma were not for me. I became anything but "nurse material." As a matter of fact, I was thinking more along the lines of an easy, rich, spoiled life—no work, but plenty of money and success. My family lived well. The world was beckoning. It became easier and easier to convince myself that nursing was not for me. What I *knew* inside *was* for me, was as far away as east and west can be.

When I was a senior in high school, I had little direction about the next step in my life. A man came and spoke to our school about airline stewardesses and the ability to help people in Africa, India, poor nations. He talked about Dr. Tom Dooley. I had read about Dr. Dooley—I admired him very much. My inner, untouched, unworldly part said, "Yes, that's it!"

And so I went to work for the airlines. Yes, I thought about helping people. But I also thought about seeing the world, glamour, riches—all of it. And "easy" … I still wanted that, too.

I married and became a mother. I loved my children, but my marriage was difficult and challenging. My easy world was not to be found. The divorce was not easy. I had no money, little skills, three babies and no hope. I moved with my three children to live with my mother and father on the East Coast.

I worked at a nearby laundry every day, long hours into the night. It was hard work, but it fed my children. And still, I wanted "the easy life."

One night, as I was looking out of my window, I saw an image of myself with a nurse's hat on my head.

The dream was back.

But how to accomplish it? I had no money, no home, three children. And the worst part? I still hated sickness, hospitals—that "smell." I couldn't even drive by a hospital without shuddering. My dream had become my weakness.

And everyone close to me said that I couldn't do it.

Well ... the journey always begins with the first step. One week later, my three children, the dog, and I were in the car and down the road, driving cross-country back to California. The trip was not easy. The old Mercedes died in Nevada. The money ran out. You know the saying: "So close, and yet so far."

A very dear friend picked us up in Nevada and brought us home. We had nothing. We slept on the floor. My youngest daughter had to have her appendix out. It was not pleasant. To add to the stress, I went over to the school and found out my pre-nursing classes were to begin in three days.

I attended the classes. Before I knew it, it was time to apply to nursing school. It was very difficult the year I applied. There were over five hundred younger women who submitted applications, and the school was going to accept only eighteen of us. I did not have much of a chance. Rigorous interviews and then the waiting.

I got in. It was a miracle.

Doors were beginning to open. I was living the reality. If God calls you, and you finally say "Yes," things begin to happen.

I loved nursing school, but it wasn't easy. I had three growing children, a mortgage, and bills to pay. Between caring for Nick, Linda, and Gig, attending classes and studying, I was working three different jobs—as an EMT with the fire department, a nurse's assistant, and writing a newspaper column for the local paper. It was non-stop ... mom, work, mom, school, mom.

I graduated from nursing school the year of my fortieth birthday. I had worked hard, graduating near the top of my class.

I was ready for the next step.

And yet ... I still was hoping for the "easy life."

I had a lot to learn.

THE PROMISE

I began to work for The Registry, a placement agency for nurses, getting experience in various hospitals and clinics with many different surgeons and excellent doctors. Larry, a successful plastic surgeon, took me under his wing and trained me well. "Katie, you must never cut corners. You must never compromise." And so on. Although a lot of people thought he was a harsh man, he was very good to me—he said it was because he liked redheads. Larry saw my children for free. I learned a lot from him. My nursing skills were in demand. I never lacked a job.

My three children were now adults, in college, and moving on with their lives.

I still had my weaknesses. I still wanted the "easy life."

But it was time.

When I became a nurse, I promised God that I would share my skills. When you promise God anything, you need to deliver.

And so, I shared my nursing skills at home and abroad. I went to Peru and Mexico with doctors, volunteering with the Flying Samaritans and other groups, working with surgeons who performed cleft palate operations for the poor in those countries. The children, the babies, the poverty, the great need ... the eye-opening experiences occurred one after another. It was heart-breaking. I was grateful to be able to help, even if it was just a little.

But that wasn't "it." I wanted more.

I had read about Mother Teresa years before. Many things she said stuck in my mind, but one particular thing kept coming back to me: "It is not by words, but by example that you put your love into action." In other words, walk your talk. I could not stop thinking about Mother and Calcutta. My being, my heart was one big desire. Mother Teresa was my idol, the person I admired most. She was in my eyes a hero, a saint, all of it.

That's it. I wanted "India."

Laurie and I had been in nursing classes together. After graduation, she joined the Missionaries of Charity—she became Sister Andrew. I went to see her in San Francisco at the Missionaries of Charity's house on Fulton Street. I told her, "Sister Andrew, what I really want to do is to go to India work with Mother Teresa." She said, "Well, go ahead. Write Mother Teresa and tell her that."

I did. I asked her if she and the Missionaries of Charity could use my help, my nursing skills. Three months later a letter arrived from India. Mother Teresa said, "Please come and see."

Another door opened. The real journey was about to begin.

THE PREPARATION

Forty-six years of preparation. Mother Teresa's invitation put things in rapid motion. I wrote back immediately. I received a letter from Sister Priscilla, who I later would learn was Mother's assistant. She sent information about places to stay and the times I could see her to begin work.

For the next several weeks, there were plans to be made, details to arrange. I didn't know anything about traveling to India. I had to research, ask questions, make calls, talk with friends, get answers.

First, there were the shots. Since this was my first trip to India, I needed a series of vaccinations—from encephalitis to cholera to typhoid. Then, there was the process of getting a visa. I also had to figure out the plane connections and make reservations. My good friend, Meena, who moved to California from India years ago, helped me by contacting her family. They planned to meet me in New Delhi before I would go on to Calcutta—and I would be able to bring much-needed medicine for Meena's father.

Finally, everything was done. I had my tickets; my bags were packed—with much-needed vitamins, medicines, and medical supplies, as well as monetary donations for the MCs and their work. I was ready to go. My dream was becoming a reality.

And the easy life?

Perhaps for the first time, I was beginning to realize that maybe, just maybe, the easy life wasn't for me.

DESIRES OF THE HEART

Mother Teresa once told me, "God will always fulfill the deepest desires of your heart. Because he's the one that put them there."

THE LETTER

MISSIONARIES OF CHARITY
54A Lower Circular Road
Calcutta 700016
India

17 October, 1992

Dear Katie,

Thank you very much for your letter. You are welcome to share in our works of love for the Poor. Come with a heart to love and hands to serve Jesus in the crippled, the abandoned, the sick and dying in anyone of our centres.

I enclose for you information a list of accommodations—they do not take reservations. On arrival you may put up at one of these till you find a more suitable place.

You can meet me at the above address between 8:30-9:00 or 5:00-6:00 p.m. daily, except Thursday and Sunday. Regarding your visa, you can come on a tourist visa and of course you would be expected to tour.

God loves you. He will reward your generous desire to serve Him in His little ones—the Poor.

God Bless you,

Sr. M. Priscilla, MC

The Journey Begins

(Excerpts from Katie's Seasons Journal—
the first trip to Calcutta)

DESTINATION: INDIA

All the planning is now in full swing. I have many feelings, some fearful, some anxious. I'm leaving the security of this country and the people I love. Somehow I know that when I come home, I will never be the same. Gig, my youngest daughter, wrote me a nice letter that I will keep forever. She wanted to make sure I knew she loved me, and she asked me to stay away from strange places. I will take her advice.

Now that we have taken off, my mind is soaring, "What's next?" Traveling seems so ominous, all the strangeness and "what-if's." I change planes or equipment in St. Louis, and then non-stop to London's Gatwick, then over to the Heathrow end of London and the Penta Hotel—wow!

The journey has begun. Only God knows what lies ahead; if I knew, I probably would never go, but then I wouldn't be doing what it seems I should do with my life. How many people have the privilege of being a nurse, and then to actually see Mother Teresa? I even have packages to hand deliver. What a privilege; it will be a high point in my life. Eileen gave me some of her homemade bread, and I have it with me. I'll have to remember to tell her that. Cathy gave me vitamins, how thoughtful. Linda R. gave up her commission—God will certainly bless her for that; I was very touched. Patricia gave me a journal, and I will write in that in New Delhi.

LONDON

On the plane to London, I got a window seat. Everything smooth so far. As soon as we take off ... I'm on my way—push back—St. Louis to London.

In flight to London, I'm thinking how simply I'm writing ... and when I arrive at my destination how complex words will have to be to describe what I shall see and do.

Arriving in Gatwick. The English are very friendly to me; the customs agent asked where I was headed. I told him to do nursing in India. He was very kind; that says a lot for England. After going through customs, I needed to get over to Terminal 1—what an ordeal, let alone very expensive, $25 for a one-hour bus ride! I ran into a very nice American man who's now made his home in Ireland (Waterford). We had a nice chat, and he was a big help.

It's so cold and damp here, but the countryside is lovely and green, and people are very polite. Waiting at Heathrow for the Penta Hotel bus seems so long. I am tired and really need a bed to lay on—to interject here, the speed link bus served hot tea; it seems so civilized.

Arrived at the Penta—a lovely place, but expensive. The room was so welcoming. Marble bathroom. I had a lovely bath, a Coke, and a five-hour nap. I walked around the hotel, very large, clean, and nice. Had the most wonderful dinner of onion soup, roll, and green salad with a mustard dressing, and a Double Diamond beer—English beer is good. Some meals stick in your mind; this will be my last fresh salad for a time ... nothing raw in India.

In the room next to mine is someone who is chanting and has kept it up all day (I heard it in my sleep). I guess I'm being prepared by

God. I can't describe it, but a definite religious chant. What energy to do that continually. Not to mention hard on the vocal cords. So, sleep—and then the long trip to India.

Didn't sleep well because of the anticipation and the unknown. Got up early, had some food, and left early for check-in. After all the rush, found out my flight is delayed three hours—not good. My anxiety increases because I anticipated having a lot of time in New Delhi. Now my luggage may get lost in the shuffle. I was planning on being met in New Delhi by Meena's sister. I was going to get rid of all this heavy stuff; now we shall see. I may get to Calcutta, but my luggage may not. Mini anxiety attack ... I toyed with the idea of getting on the TWA flight going home. After all this, it just is scary being so far from home.

The delay at Heathrow lasted almost four hours; it seemed endless. If feels so strange; now I am very much the foreigner. I'm so glad my friends are praying for me. I'm really going to miss my children and security and safety. Maybe God wanted me to take this trip to make me realize certain things—like how blessed I am. I do know this, but I now feel like a small fish in a very large ocean. In some ways I am afraid of everything, yet strangely very brave; I'm also afraid of being a coward. Ah, but to go and see Mother Teresa and learn from her and the other Sisters ... of course, I shall come home safely. How could I not go? We Americans have so many things at our disposal; I learned in Peru just how rich I am. I imagine I shall learn double that lesson in Calcutta.

It's hard at these times to be by myself. That's the turn my life has taken. I think that it's in anxious, trying times like these that our heart-aches haunt us the most.

NEW DELHI

The plane ride to New Delhi was smooth. But I must say, the food was AWFUL! And everyone smoked. I slept sitting up for three hours and I tell you, I look it and feel it. We arrive in New Delhi. I did not see Meena's family at the airport, and I feel bad.

It seems it's going to be either me or my luggage that makes the plane to Calcutta. The customs people assure me my luggage will get on; another Indian lady has the same problem. It's so stressful. Anyway, I have no choice. On the ground, the Calcutta flight waited, thank God ... I feel taken care of.

My assigned seat is next to a man who owns a tanning factory in Calcutta, and guess who his neighbor is: the Mother House of Mother Teresa. God's planning is amazing! This man was very kind, informative, gave me the details I needed to fill in those holes, like what NOT to do, etc., and how to make my plans, change planes/trains, the differences between Calcutta and New Delhi, etc. He says he thinks Mother Teresa is out of town—I hope not.

Anyway, here I sit in New Delhi, the plane is delayed three hours here also. Soon I'll be in Calcutta and, hopefully, lodging will not be a problem!

BREAKFAST EN ROUTE TO CALCUTTA

It's Friday, February 12. We have taken off. The sun is coming up. The breakfast was served, but I can't eat it. This is not a good sign; round breads and some sort of lamb … and it looked like the hair of the animal was still on it. Even if I was starving, I believe my throat would have slammed shut because of the smell alone.

WHITE TENNIS SHOES

Why would anybody wear white tennis shoes to Calcutta, India?

Because they did not know better—someone like me. On my first trip I thought I would need comfortable shoes—white tennis shoes, really white. I bought them before leaving for Calcutta.

Landing in Calcutta, the first smudge appeared on the first step out of the plane door and down the old metal staircase ... then walking across the runway; again and again, areas of dirt. Going through customs was hot, humid; dirty water on the floor. Now the white shoes are light gray.

Out the door through a mud puddle. Still dark outside; into a cab. Oil spilled inside the cab on the floor. Now the shoes were black and filthy and greasy. Half way to the city, first trip, a flat tire. Out of the cab, into a pile of muck.

Arriving in the city, the other tire went flat right in the middle of a colony of people who were lepers living together in the streets. Out of the car, another pile of muck.

First day, first two hours. Now new black, filthy, muddy, greasy tennis shoes.

FIRST IMPRESSIONS

My worst fears were realized at the airport. My bags didn't make it. Another woman and man are in the same predicament. Yet I feel peace that they will turn up, God willing. Thankfully I brought a change of clothing in my backpack.

Now on to feelings. What can I say to describe Calcutta? It's very foreign. There is an unusual feeling in the air. This part of the earth looks and feels different. My first impression quite simply is this: "It's lovely." I don't mean the poverty or dirt, but I feel better I'm here. This place on earth is where I am, and I know in my heart I'll never repeat these feeling or steps and, of course, never be the same.

I mailed Meena's father's medicine from the airport. The lady at the airport said it would arrive in two days. He needs this for his eyes and the pressure. Then, on to the Airport Ashok Hotel. Need to find rest.

They have a room and, of course, it's more expensive. The Maitre'd of the hotel looked at me and tacked on another $30 (US). I went to my room and turned the water on, and was welcomed by a multitude of cockroaches jumping—no, flying—out of the sink. Families of cockroaches. I guess I have no choice until I leave and lodge near the Mother House and get my bags from the airport. I made my calls to home. How wonderful to speak to my children Linda, Nick, and Gig—very comforting.

I called Meena's brother and sister in New Delhi. I will stay with them at the end of February and early March on my return trip home. They were disappointed about the delays as they had waited and announced my name at the airport in New Delhi. What a small tragedy.

Cab trip into town for supplies. Back to the hotel. I slept very soundly for ten hours. My body, spirit, and soul are tired. My day will be beginning soon, and who knows what February 13th holds for me.

What a trip to come to Calcutta. How scary. I know not one soul, but I clutch my letter from Sister Priscilla telling me where to go, when to see her.

Here I am. Thank you, God.

EIGHT DAYS IN CALCUTTA

Journal Entry: February 21, 1993

Eight days have passed … this is the first time I've been able to write since arriving in Calcutta. It was so personal and overwhelming that words didn't seem to come to describe what I was seeing and feeling.

Calcutta is a hundred times worse than I had ever imagined; yet, I also have never felt so close to God. I have seen so many things; how can I ever be the same?

Even though I served as a nurse in Peru, Mexico, and my own country, I was unprepared for India. The extreme poverty and dirt were overwhelming. A sea of humanity living in the streets. Each day you see the sickness, disease, poverty, hunger, death … the children, the babies, the elderly, the crippled. Each day you experience a mixture of emotions, trying to make sense of the differences in a culture that is not at all like our own.

Each day you live a lifetime.

If I were to die tomorrow, I feel as though coming and being with Mother Teresa and sharing this work has completed my life. I see all my faults here; it's so clear how selfish and self-centered I am. That can change with God's help. I know I cannot do it myself.

Father Joseph, the pastor of St. Theresa's in Calcutta, said none of us is alike, and God made us this way so we could do the job he has asked each of us to do. So, in spite of all my shortcomings, God still asks me to do the work he has planned for me.

Calcutta is hell itself.

If Mother Teresa and the Sisters were not here, the misery, suffering, and starvation would be unbearable.

Mother Teresa, the Missionaries of Charity, and Calcutta

◆

The First Time

MEETING MOTHER TERESA

Coming to the Mother House in India was a heart's desire come true.

The taxi dropped me off in the heart of Calcutta. I walked down the narrow lane with my letter in hand, looking up at each large concrete building I passed for the address of the convent. The number 54A was clearly visible as I came to the Mother House, and right above it, Mother Teresa, M.C. The sign said that she was "in." I stopped and rang the bell.

Entering the convent that first day, I could not control the tears. They were happy tears. God was so close and present. I sat on a bench outside a drawn curtain. Mother Teresa was inside. She came out, and I saw one of the tiniest women ever. She moved very quickly—I soon learned she wastes no time. She walked by me; it took my breath away. She stopped, turned around, and came over, took one of my hands, looked deeply into my eyes and said, "Welcome."

I was speechless. I couldn't move. Her gaze held mine. I just kept on looking into her eyes.

My first impression was that she looks 16 years old—the look in her eyes, so full of life. And her hands—the softest hands I had ever felt. Many of us who have known Mother and have been touched by her have all said, "those beautiful, soft hands."

The next thing I knew, she was gone.

But the fragrance lingered. God's Perfume ...

My new nickname for Mother Teresa.

INTRODUCTION TO KALIGHAT

I'm not sure how long afterwards it was—I was still in shock—a Sister came over to me with a big smile and said: "You are a nurse. We would like you to begin working at Kalighat." Kalighat is the first hospital Mother Teresa opened in Calcutta for the destitute and dying. The building was donated to Mother Teresa by the government of India. Sister Priscilla was Mother Teresa's "right hand." She knew what the MC's needs were, where they were, how you could fill them. I was still holding her letter in my hand.

She looked me up and down. She saw how dirty I was, just from traveling from my hotel and walking to the convent. I think she also saw that I was perhaps a bit "soft." She added, "And you should stay just down the road here at the Circular Hotel; it's close by the Mother House."

Kalighat. I didn't know anything about Kalighat before I came to India.

I would like to say I had no difficulty and went directly to work there and had a joyful attitude. But that was not the case.

The conditions at Kalighat were appalling. The smells and the suffering and the heat were beyond anything I had ever encountered. So many people were dying and brought there after years and years of starvation and abuse. They had been born and lived in the streets and, if not for Mother, would have died there also.

My first task was to bring water from a cistern in a dark cement room. Then I was to begin bathing the ladies. Looking into that cold, filthy water, I knew I could not do it. I went off to a corner and said, "Lord, please forgive me. I <u>cannot</u> do this. I want to go home."

I know that the Sisters saw me go off, and I know that they prayed for me. Well, I came back. Unstable and shaky, I washed more starving, broken, lice-infested bodies of women than I could count. I was functioning under God's grace and mercy.

That was my first day at Kalighat.

It was the beginning of what would make my life never again the same.

KALIGHAT DAYS

I spent many long days working at Kalighat. I learned so much each day. So much.

I remember the first time I met Sister Luke. She was in charge of Kalighat. What a presence. And so gifted. Sister Luke taught me a lot in short order. She could start an IV on anyone. She trained me in her method. We became fast friends.

I was worried a lot at Kalighat on this first trip. Was I caring for the patients properly? Were they okay? Was I doing things the "right" way? Sister Luke assured me and told me a story.

After she was first assigned as the head of Kalighat, she also was worried about her patients. She was responsible for all of them. During the MC's daily rest period, she would peek out from behind the curtains every five minutes to check on the men and women to make sure everything was fine. She couldn't rest. She cared too much.

Another example of putting love into action.

SHISHU BHAVAN: "THE TEST"

Shishu Bhavans—Mother's homes for the children.

After learning about the Shishu Bhavan in Calcutta, I knew that I would want to work there, too. But this had to be approved by Sister Marcellina. She was in charge. Anyone who wanted to work there had to pass "the test."

I didn't know what the test was.

When I went to speak to Sister Marcellina about helping, a child had just been found. She was two years old and appeared half that age. She was tiny and very weak; she could not even stand. Sister Marcellina handed her to me and asked if I could please feed her.

My heart hurt so bad. I wanted to just break down and cry and never stop. The unshed tears stayed in my eyes. They did not drop.

I passed. I found out later that I almost failed. What was the test? NO TEARS.

Two days later, this beautiful little girl was standing and walking. And, two weeks later, she was running everywhere.

Sister Marcellina and I became good friends, and I later told her, "I saved all my tears for the trip on the way home."

I'm sure that in some place—Bangkok, Tokyo, London—people are still talking about the woman who just sat waiting for her plane, crying. Unshed tears saved up for the ride home.

Good tears—cleansing, happy tears.

Thankful tears. For the gift of life … for Mother Teresa and the Sisters.

For their very special calling.

PLEASE CAN YOU HELP?

With each passing day, I was meeting more and more of the Sisters. They would stop me, and say, "Please can you help me with …?" I was happy to help. I wanted to help—it was the reason I had come to Calcutta. And, as time went on and I saw how much the Sisters gave of themselves, it made me want to give all the more. Mother and the MCs made me feel so welcome. They were more than friends. They made feel like I was a part of their "family."

I very quickly learned that the MCs were grateful for any medical training a volunteer brought to Calcutta. These skills were badly needed. And word got around fast. I began to understand why they were happy that an experienced well-trained nurse had come—not just me, but any nurse.

My nursing skills were being used to the hilt.

God was making sure that I kept my promise.

WELCOME TO THE DISPENSARY

That was how I met Sister Andrea and Sister Shanta … and learned about "the Dispensary."

Sister Andrea and Sister Shanta are two very special MCs. I am privileged to know them. They are opposites in personality, nature, and in ways of doing things; but many years ago, Mother Teresa joined them together to work at "the Dispensary," the MC's central storehouse of critical medicine and medical supplies in Calcutta. That was that. Two opposites became a single unit, a team—one in mind and heart, working for God.

The Dispensary is located in the side courtyard of the Shishu Bhavan. From this site, the Sisters serve the medical needs of hundreds of the poor daily. Sister Andrea is in charge. She is one of three MCs in Calcutta who are doctors. Sister Shanta is responsible for everything that goes in and out of the Dispensary. She is not a doctor, but everyone does what she says—she has a very commanding presence. Sister Shanta is the best organizer I know.

And, nothing at the Dispensary is wasted.

For example, take the old, used wound dressings. If they were not shredded and still sturdy, they were boiled and sterilized, re-wrapped, and re-used. I had the great pleasure of helping the Sisters at the Dispensary with this task. It was fun. I laughed. We laughed.

I had visions of my colleagues at home saying, "You did what???" Well, yes, I did! Recycled old dressings with great joy.

I loved being with the Sisters.

They radiated joy ... great joy ... in the midst of all the suffering.

NEW FRIENDS

Harry, Andy, Janine, Esther, Auntie Ella ...

Just some of the very special people I met on my first trip to Calcutta. The volunteers.

The volunteers who came to work with Mother and the MCs are of all ages, from places around the world, each with our own background, our own story. We all wanted, in some way, to help.

There is something unusual, exceptional—how to describe it?—about working together in Calcutta, in serving the poorest of the poor. You may be as different as different can be, but day in and day out, you witness the oppression, the suffering, the extreme poverty. Deep, unspoken bonds begin to form. I imagine that it's something like medics working together during a war. You have to experience it to understand it.

After a long hard day of work, a few of us might meet over a meal, exhausted, sharing pieces of our lives, recounting the sorrows and joys of our day. We would laugh, we would cry.

I knew these friendships would last a lifetime, whether or not we ever saw each other again, although we often did.

Take Harry for example ...

HARRY AND THE BUS

I loved Harry, but I did not like Harry right away. I met Harry on a #39A bus ride to Kalighat.

At the time, I was shell-shocked by India. The smells, the sounds, the sights. I was questioning everything I was seeing. I was a raw, open wound, absorbing strangeness of every sort. East and West were so different—noise, disease, pollution, death, poverty, fear. Definitely overload.

And then, on the bus was this smiling man with a huge head of curly, black hair—a white man with an Afro—that's what I saw. Harry was Armenian. He was friendly, smiling, helpful, and looked to me like one of the biggest, most foolish salesmen I'd ever seen.

I thought he was an idiot.

Riding the bus to Kalighat from the Mother House, you have about twenty minutes of a rocky, wild ride from the center of town. Then you get dumped off at the stop, and you need to be *fast*, because your hand is barely off the pole, and the bus is gone. You may still be hanging onto the pole, but the bus is GONE.

After the traumatic bus ride, you walk through a huge marketplace on your way to Kalighat. I asked about Harry—he was well ahead running to Kalighat to work. Danielle said, "Harry is an American doctor." My first thought was that this person cannot be a doctor. Harry did NOT fit the mold—couldn't be true. But it was, and you know what? He was a darn good doctor.

Harry was a walking example of God's love. I was honored to be able to work with him often—on my first trip, and when I returned.

Harry gave up two years of his life to India.

And then? Harry decided to give the rest of his life to God.

He's becoming a priest.

A calling within a calling.

THE MISSIONARIES OF CHARITY BROTHERS

The MC Brothers have a special place in my heart.

The Brothers serve the poor throughout Calcutta ... at Kalighat, the leper colony at Titagarh, and countless other places. The Brothers don't wear habits like the Sisters. Many of them wear punjavis—loose, billowy pants and shirts—very Indian. Some dress more Western. But they all have one thing in common: they wear a simple cross. This is the mark that they are Brothers, that they have given their lives to Jesus and the Missionaries of Charity.

I met many Brothers at Kalighat on my first trip. They were all hard working and kind. "Wound care" seemed to be their specialty. But when I think of the Brothers and that first trip, there is something that always plays in my mind ...

Sunday music at Kalighat.

Every Sunday there is a Mass at Kalighat. It begins with the Brothers playing small organs and drums. And they sing as they play. Beautiful, rhythmic, peaceful sounds.

Music for the ears ... and the heart.

MOTHER'S TOUCH

I've often thought if you are meant to be a nurse, you carry an extra gene. It's called "The Nurse Gene." It carries "big burdens." Everything and everybody, every illness, every accident—we are somehow responsible for all of it, or we caused it, or could have prevented it.

I had carried this gene all my life. But on my first trip to Calcutta, something happened.

It was my last day in Calcutta. I was flying to Israel for nine days before returning home. Mother was leaving the next day for Hong Kong.

India and Israel had developed diplomatic ties. Many dignitaries were in Calcutta, and most were at the Mother House. They wanted to meet this famous nun.

After the prayer service that evening, I wanted Mother Teresa's final blessing before I left Calcutta. The Sisters told me that before everything ends, I should run out and then I could catch Mother. Well, I did ... and so did about fifty others with the same intention. I could see that it wasn't going to happen, but that was okay. And then ...

Mother was probably about twenty feet away from me. She looked at me and said, "*What do you want?*" I said, "Your blessing, Mother." She came towards me. It was like the Red Sea parting. She stretched out both hands. I put my head down, and she touched my head with both hands. I felt, I sensed, I knew something marvelous had just occurred.

The nurse "gene" and the big burdens?

Gone. Taken away by God through Mother's hands.

My skills now could now be used and given to the fullest … without any hindrances.

The healing had begun.

LIVING A LIFETIME EACH DAY

My first trip to Calcutta … three weeks with Mother and the MCs.

In some ways, it was a whirlwind, a blur. Everything happened so fast. And yet, every sight, every situation, every person remains vivid—entrenched in my mind, my memory, my heart.

My first day at Kalighat was the beginning. I was, I am forever changed. Each day in Calcutta was a day of mercy. I wanted to cry all the time … the extreme poverty, starvation, sickness. Babies too weak to move for the lack of food. But then the joy in seeing them improve, their eyes becoming bright, the smiles—truly one of the greatest treasures.

Each day in Calcutta, you live a lifetime.

There are so many stories and memories. It would take years to tell them all … the people I met, the miracles I saw. When I returned to India to work again, I was privileged to be treated as one of the Sisters. They took me to so many places and taught me so much.

And always the simple message: Love one another. And put your love into action.

God has a plan for each of us.

A call.

In my case, if I had known what I would see or experience in Calcutta on that first trip, I may have said "no."

And I would have missed the beginning of the best part of my life.

May we all have the courage and grace to say "yes" to the calling.

ENJOY AND SHARE

During my first visit to Calcutta, I began to feel disturbed. I felt guilt about all that I possessed, even though I lived simply. But when compared with India, there was no comparison.

One day, I was at the Mother House and fortunate to catch Mother alone. Without asking to speak with her—it's as if she already knows—she made room for me on the bench. I said, "Mother, I feel as though I have so much. I am very torn."

Mother's response? Simple and direct. Her words always got right to the heart of the matter.

"Where you are is where God has placed you. Enjoy what you have. God only asks that you share."

Sharing and giving away ... lightening the load ... disposing oneself for total giving ... and total receiving.

The beginning of the path to true freedom.

LETTER FROM SR. ANDREA—JULY 7, 1993

Dear Katie,

Thanks for the big box full of precious stuff! Yes, we received everything safely—especially the IV, IM needles are like gold! And I was so grateful for the baby oil and powder—you remembered the kids out in the village! Well, we've starting to give them a BATH right on the spot—so we need the oil to rub them down gently afterwards as they are often COVERED with sores! Next time you come please carry some soap and towels, we use 3-4 or even more towels every Saturday (in spite of the "sharing"—what to do!) And we need the Q-tips so much, because many of the kids have ear infections with pus running out. Our team got a new doctor—sister, a trained pediatrician—what a gift from God! I say—the thoughtfulness of Jesus ...

We're looking forward to having you here again, please God. You can help also with some suggestions—we always need to improve. How was Independence Day? Our Mother came back from Rome and Ireland, a bit tired but full of zeal for CHINA! I'm sure she'll take Jesus in there soon! Sr. Priscilla is doing fine....

And may you, too, experience deep joy in belonging to Him—the best friend we could ask for!

God bless you Katie,
Sister Andrea, MC

A Happy Return

ANOTHER VISIT

I'm rather numb. I think I'm overwhelmed, but I'm too tired to really know my condition. I'm most grateful to God for my safe, rather uneventful journey. In the past, getting to India has not been smooth.

I'm so very happy to be here—to be back in Calcutta. In some way, it's as if I only just left yesterday. To be plunked down in the middle of India with the noise, smell, and the total chaos is very extreme. Such a paradox how in all this hell, God is so close. And the Indian people—so poor, so lacking in material things, but so filled with peace and joy, so rich in the things that matter.

I have only arrived and Sister Andrea saved me a room at the Circular Hotel. I have a full force, head-on view of Circular Road—horns honking, streetcars, buses, trucks, endless streams of people.

I went to the Mother House to thank God for my safe arrival and for all the supplies that arrived with me. Mother Teresa and Sister Shanti were there when I went into the chapel. Sister Shanti said, "Speak to Mother and get her blessing; you are suffering from jet lag."

So I went. But Mother was speaking to Sister Ann from New Jersey. I got up to leave because I didn't want to interrupt. Mother saw me and said, "Sit down. I'll be seeing you right away." So, down I sit.

Mother comes over to me and says, "Let's get out of the draft." To sit next to this saint and get her blessing and to have her speak to me—truly an honor and thrill. Words cannot convey my soul and spirit … they are singing with great joy! She carries God's presence like perfume … it's wonderful to be with her.

She playfully strokes my face and holds my head, also lovingly holds my hand—her hands have not changed, they are as soft as ever. If it's possible, Mother has become smaller; her spine has shrunk more. Her pain must be very severe, but you would never know it.

Sister Ann asks for my help—maybe I can go to her small village. When I say, "Of course," Mother says, "You are a beautiful woman." I know what she means, but I think I might have blushed anyway. She shoves me playfully and says, "Go sleep and come and see me tomorrow." I told her I brought many things—some supplies and money from people at home. She thanked me and smiled. I left and went to the hotel to sleep.

With God's Perfume surrounding me.

GOD'S PERFUME

"God's Perfume" quickly became my nickname for Mother Teresa.

Perfume ... it surrounds, inhabits, and leaves a residue, a scent. Pleasant, touches the senses.

Unless we live it, feel it, experience it—we cannot express it fully in words.

God's Perfume ... Mother Teresa. Before she came into a room, God would lead her and God would follow her. He would leave this scent as a beautiful experience, costly perfume. Mother's perfume ... God's presence. It awakened the spirit and soul. It contained the essence of God.

Money cannot buy it. But it costs.

All you have to do is say "yes" to God, and you and I can have our own perfume—God's presence surrounding us, just as he surrounded Mother Teresa.

The finest gift penetrating your heart and soul as only God can do, filling all those spaces only he can fill ... spaces meant only for him.

God's Perfume. Mother Teresa carried this fragrance. She was "a carrier of God's love." She used these words to describe herself and the Sisters ... "carriers of God's love."

And me?

I was fortunate to be in their presence.

NOW YOU GO AND SHARE

Mother Teresa was very playful and had a great sense of humor. If I had a question in my heart, I knew Mother would have a simple word that would clarify everything. She always had heavenly answers.

I was at the Mother House. I had a question for Mother, and I was fortunate this day to literally run into her. Mother was always on a mission; idleness was not a word she knew. This time she was on her way to London. The car was downstairs to take her to the airport. I was two steps below her, and so we were almost eye-to-eye—Mother was very tiny. I'm 5'4', and Mother Teresa's head reached my armpits.

Without having even asked my question, she shook her finger at me, "Now I have been sharing with you every day, now you go and share." Then she gave me that playful slap on the side of my head.

Okay Mother. You answered my question. I will share my memories and stories of you, the Sisters, Calcutta, everything …

Shared words, shared wisdom, shared experiences.

With the hope that some may benefit.

WRITE WHAT YOU HAVE SEEN

Mother told me to share.

And just before I was leaving to go back home, Sister Shanta gave me a diary. She looked at me and said, "Write what you have seen here."

Mother Teresa and Sister Shanta had given me permission to put my dream into action.

They always seemed to know. They knew that I desired to share, that I would write about it all—the joy, the pain, the fun, the growth, the challenges, the sadness, the miracles, the people, my friends, and so much more.

I would put it all in the diary.

I would obey Mother Teresa and Sister Shanta.

May God help me to find the right words.

A DROP IN THE OCEAN

"How can you stand seeing and doing all that stuff in India?"

I get asked this question all the time … usually before I leave for India or when I arrive back home.

I ask the same question of myself, and my answer is in two parts: I can't stand it; and I don't like seeing it. It's made worse by the fact that I don't like sickness, dirt, bugs, starvation, disease, and all the other indignities that accompany being poor.

And, although I always wanted to be a nurse, I hated trauma, blood, vomit. I'd even go out of my way to avoid driving by a hospital.

They say God likes to use our weaknesses to make us strong or give us the strength to do as he asks. In my case, this is an understatement. I needed a lot of grace … and mercy, too.

If I had not said "yes" to God's call for my life, I truly would have missed the best of everything.

Feeding a hungry baby and watching the strength come back … easing the pain of being helpless and dying alone … seeing pain and knowing I can do something to help. Even if it's one person, one child … one moment can change everything.

As Mother says, "We must do small things with great love. We might feel that what we are doing is insignificant, like a drop in the ocean. But if that one drop weren't there, I think the ocean would be missing something. It would be less because of that missing drop."

Mother Teresa knew:

"Each drop makes a difference."

The Missionaries of
Charity—Living the Call

THE MISSION

With Mother Teresa, living the call boiled down to "love."

Spreading the fragrance.

Mother always said, "Love must be put into action." The Missionaries of Charity are the carriers of God's love. They carry with them this love and it shows in all of them—loving, joyful, peaceful spirits. God has called each one of them to his service, to love him in the "poorest of the poor." As Mother always said, "God loves the world through you and me." There are millions and millions of people in the world, in India, without food or love. God called Mother Teresa and all of the MCs to help—to give love and more—to see to it that no one is ever turned away.

Mother never began the day without Mass and Communion. She said that without this, she could not function and do the work that God called her to do. She said that God's work cannot be forced; it must come from above.

How to begin? "We must do small things with great love."

Mother Teresa walked with God, and she carried his presence with her.

If one were ever to doubt that God existed, I believe that after being in the presence of Mother Teresa and the Sisters, this doubt would vanish.

MOTHER'S POVERTY

The MCs own nothing but two saris—their habits: one to be worn, and one extra when the other needs to be cleaned or mended. The cloth for all the habits and clothing is woven by the lepers at Titagarh—the leper colony just outside of Calcutta. The Sisters willingly live like the people they serve—simply and without any luxuries. This is the way Mother wanted it: her vow of poverty.

Sister Andrea told me Mother was afraid of compromising her poverty by having anything the poor did not have—even down to a new sari or a more comfortable kneeling cushion. No compromise. She stayed as poor as those she served. Even a glass of juice in the morning, rich in potassium for her heart—the poor could not afford it, so neither would Mother want it. Sister Andrea would say, "Mother, for the love of God, please drink your juice." Then Mother drank the juice—"for the love of God."

Many people have asked, "Why no washing machine, no modern conveniences?" This, too, is a part of Mother's poverty. Her community, her homes, those who help would also remain poor, like the poor that she and the Sisters serve.

Take Kalighat for example.

The washing and the dishes are all done by hand. And none of it is easy. But the conversations and the friendships, the bonds, and even marriages have all come from being together during this work. From this, the volunteers have been changed; no one goes away without these changes, and no one goes home unaffected by the simple way of life and the sense of giving and receiving. And this is true, I believe, even if they don't see it at the time. Bonds formed and bad habits changed; so much good from the toil and drudgery of a "social hour" of work ... every day hard, hard work.

Thank you, Mother, for not compromising your vow of poverty.

And for showing us what is really important.

IT'S IN THE FACES

There was one particular Sunday at Kalighat I remember very well ...

Many Sisters were upstairs in the chapel in prayer. They were visiting from Tengra, one of the MC's houses a little ways outside of Calcutta. Tengra is a Missionary of Charity house where the Sisters study and pray. Mother used to send the Sisters there once a year for a time of retreat. Tengra is part of the Sisters' formation for one year, both the contemplative and the active Sisters. Afterwards, the active Sisters often received their work assignments.

Sister Paelin, one of the assistants at Kalighat, told me that forty-five sisters were there that day. Very special. Suddenly, I heard the sound, "Katie." I turned around and there was Sister Shanta, hands on her hips, scowling at me. Then she laughed. I was so happy to see her. When I arrived at the Mother House, I was told that I probably wouldn't see her this trip ... that she was at Tengra.

Then I heard laughter and talking. I turned and saw all of the Sisters descending the stairs. Each face was different, but each joyful. Each face had a look, a glow, God's torch of love burning in her soul. Constant prayer ... it showed, it burst through.

One sign at the Mother House reads: "Joy on the face is preaching without preaching."

The Missionary of Charity Sisters—living their call, every day.

The faces cannot lie.

LEARN OF ME

There is something special about each MC, each Brother and Sister and priest.

They radiate goodness, holiness, and so much more. It's in them.

I was assigned many times at Kalighat to show wound care to a new Brother, but they always taught me more than I could ever teach them. They wanted to know everything that would help make things better for the person treated.

One year, a particular Brother was assigned to me, and I think he did not want to be. We ended up becoming great friends. I admired him so much for his humility. He would say, "Dear sister, I am so inadequate. Please teach me everything you know." And I would say, "Dear Brother, I want to be more like you."

I pray for him each day.

And I still want to be more like him.

TRUE WISDOM

Thousands of Missionaries of Charity around the world. And each one has a story. Like Sister Andrea and Sister Shanta.

On Sister Andrea's feast day one year, the priest gave a talk at Mass about how she sacrificed a life of luxury and prestige for service to God.

Sister Andrea grew up in Germany. As a student in the early 1950's, she read a magazine article about Mother Teresa and Calcutta. It struck her that this was truly what she wanted to do with her life. She told her father of her dream. He was saddened. But he gave the consent. They took a train to Belgium, then a ship around the coast of Africa to Bombay, and finally a train ride to Calcutta. I can only imagine how hard it was for her father to leave her in such a strange, noisy, dirty city, but he did. He gave away his daughter, and she gave her life to God and the MCs.

After Mass that day, Sister Andrea said to the priest, "Father, the things of the world are a burden and a hindrance." Sister Andrea is truly free. She had no doubts about what she gave up. Nothing, as compared to everything.

Sister Shanta told me that when she joined the MCs, Mother Teresa gave her the name "Shanta." It literally means "peaceful." Sister said, "Mother, I'm not a peaceful soul." Mother Teresa's answer? "You will be before you go home to God."

Sister Shanta grew up in India. She has many brothers and sisters. Sister Shanta has a very strong presence. You always do or will find a way to get done what she tells you or asks you to do. She carries a lot of authority; God made her in a very special way. Andy says that Sister

Shanta is like an "old battleship." She's tough, but soft ... a very powerful combination.

Both Sister Andrea and Sister Shanta are always working, or on their way to accomplish something that needs to be done. One day, when I reminded Sister Shanta about the daily rest, she said, "We will rest when we get to heaven."

Somehow, knowing them both ...

Sister Shanta and Sister Andrea will be working in heaven, too.

Six Powerful Words

Gary came to Calcutta many years ago as a volunteer.

He never left. He became a Missionary of Charity priest.

And now, Father Gary is the head of the priests of the Missionaries of Charity around the world.

I had the gift of knowing Father Gary well.

One particular year, I went to Calcutta with a wound on my heart. It was ever present, and it was something that had affected me very deeply and emotionally. I was speaking to Father Gary and began telling him of my pain and the emotions attached to it. It became a confession.

He said many things to me to begin the healing process. Some were not easy to hear. "You must pray for this person; in praying you will forgive; in forgiving, you will begin a process on the long road to forgetting. Leave them in God's hands. You need not seek them out nor avoid them. Pray even when you don't feel like it."

So, I began the process. Forgiving, forgetting, praying. It was a journey, but I knew I was much better off in God's hands.

I will never forget Father Gary's parting words to me: "Your penance and your part in this process is to 'pray for our poor in India.'"

Six powerful words.

My problems and feelings really were quite small compared to what the poor suffer and endure each day in India. I never forgot that.

Now, whenever I start to feel sorry for myself for any reason, I remember Father Gary's words ... six powerful words.

And I pray for the poor in India ... especially the children.

JOY

On the blackboard at the Mother House in Calcutta are these words:

Joy is a net by which we catch souls.
If we are perfectionists, that net gets snagged
and we become people pleasers,
not God pleasers.

The MCs live in the midst of difficulties; hardships every day … under conditions that many would say are far from perfect. They know the secret.

Joy doesn't come from being perfectionists, or trying to make things "perfect."

Joy comes from a heart filled with true love. A heart that is peaceful amidst the trials because nothing can bother it. A heart that finds its strength not in itself or trying to please others, but in him who alone gives us strength.

The MCs *are* joy.

It's easy to get caught in this net.

And once you are, you never want to be set free.

The Face of Jesus

Do Not Be Afraid

I'm very proud of my daughter, Linda. Her goal to become a doctor came about from a trip we made together to Calcutta.

Of all my three children, Nick, Linda, and Margaret ("Gig"), Linda is the most delicate. In 1996, after she graduated from college she said to me, "Mom, I want to do something decent with my life. When you go to India in December, I'm going, too."

Oh Lord, NO, please, not my most fragile child. I know India. It's harsh, I can't prepare her. The smells alone, the heat, she could get really sick. The strangeness. Nope, she can't do it. What if … what if she gets sick or hurt? Why can't I just be normal and stay home?

Well, God had other plans. He knows all our weaknesses, and he can use them to make us strong. Linda wanted to put her love into action … to "walk the talk."

And when God calls our children, he cares for them most tenderly.

Linda reacted worse than I thought, and we had not even landed in Calcutta. As we waited to identify our luggage in New Delhi, the smell of phenol hit and she almost fainted. Not a good sign. The conditions in Calcutta frightened my daughter. Her adjustment was as difficult, if not worse, than my first trip. I was very protective of her.

One morning, very early, I could not go outside. Some days the air is so polluted you feel as though you are chewing the air, not breathing it. I needed a break. Linda wanted to be with the MCs for Mass, which is early in the morning. I prayed as she left, "God, take care of her." She walked out alone in the dark pre-dawn hours … afraid. But soon, never again to be the same.

Leaving the safety of our hotel, she began the short walk to the convent. The streets were dark and still quiet. Coming toward her was a dark form dressed in filthy rags. She told me later that she was very afraid. When he was getting closer, she was going to turn and run. But he spoke to her, gently and softly. And in perfect English. "Do not be afraid." As he said this, she said all her fears left her. She turned to thank him, but no one was there.

Linda was never afraid in India again.

I relayed this story to Sister Shanta a few days later, and she said, "Oh, Katie, don't you know that many times Jesus dresses himself as our poor and comes to comfort and console us."

I have no doubt who met my daughter in the street that day. God took care of my child, and he did in a life-changing way. All her fears were taken away—stripped, gone, vanished.

Jesus became real to her. She began to understand.

When we fall in love, we lose all fear; we become brave. Linda went from a fear-filled person to a fearless faith-filled person. It was an immense gift.

The scientific mind was transformed and renewed into a faith-filled one ... just like that—going to church, seeking God and his path ... wanting to become a doctor, to help people. She surrendered her fear, and in turn God gained another heart ... and another set of hands and feet to serve.

God's work is never done, and each of us has a special and unique task to be accomplished.

May we meet God on our road so that we can go on his journey—together—to complete our task.

THE BANANA BOY

I watched a young boy, probably 8 or 9, about 7:30 at night walking up Halim Galem Street. He had a burlap bag and he was picking through the filthy garbage.

His shorts were orange, but were so dirty they were gray-orange, and his t-shirt was gray. All his clothing was full of holes. Even his burlap bag had holes. He wasn't begging and he did not even notice me. He was just intent on finding something in the garbage. My heart felt like it had rocks in it. I ached so much for him.

Mother's reminder: "We serve Jesus in the distressing disguise of the poor."

If I could have, I would have bought that boy anything, but he was moving and searching so quickly. I only had time to buy four bananas and then pray I could find him. I prayed and ran up the street. I shall never forget his eyes and the way he looked at me, not wanting to accept, but perhaps thinking of the hunger at home ... foraging for garbage.

The distressing disguise.

There is for me nothing more heartbreaking than when a child is hungry or lost or alone. I do not want this for anyone, but especially not for an innocent child born into this life eating scraps if and where he can find them. I do not want to see this "distressing disguise," but I do.

My young banana boy is one of so many, not only in India, but everywhere in our world.

When people ask me, "How can you bear this?" I tell them that I can't. It tears me apart.

But I can do something, even if it might not be much.

Even if it is only four bananas.

A drop in the ocean.

DO IT ALL FOR JESUS

It really is impossible to chart each day in India as so much happens here. But to try, I sometimes compress many such days into one. At the same time, I feel I do not want to degrade in any way or ever take lightly the suffering I see of these poor people.

My patients at Kalighat are a gift to me and I pray that I take good care of them: respectfully, quietly, never shaming them by my facial expressions or my manner, as many situations and smells can be quite overwhelming and overpowering.

Often I think of what Mother says, "Do it all for Jesus," and the worms that I take from wounds and sores, or the boils wiped, are the body of Christ.

I will do it then with love.

And God already knows that it's for him.

Life in Calcutta

FRESH AIR

When I leave Calcutta, my heart is torn—half wants to stay forever, the other half longs for home, never to return again. I miss my family, my friends, clean air, going to the water tap and turning it on for a drink of water. Such a simple, matter of fact thing at home—getting a drink of water. In Calcutta you need to be very sure it has been boiled or bottled correctly. Otherwise, you may be sick, or worse … you might acquire a life-long affliction.

Fresh, clean air is forever to me a huge gift. The air pollution in Calcutta, how can I describe this accurately? The air has a presence of its own. You can actually see what you are breathing in—huge black droplets of garbage from street debris being burned by people living on the streets, dried dung being burned in the early morning to keep the babies warm or to boil water or cook food. Walking across the street during traffic, exhaust fumes from the diesel fuels being burned by the taxis and cars.

All this combined is a disaster for the lungs and respiratory system. I have friends who have asthma who come to Calcutta in spite of their own afflictions … for love of the poor. With the bad air and the dirt, these are very brave souls. It could be their own demise, but they would rather work and give of themselves than not chance it. This is courage.

My skin is very fair. Walking one block in Calcutta, my skin has a fine gray mist. And my nose openings have become black holes from breathing. But I wasn't alone. We all suffered together. This is all a part of the initiation of India—only a small part.

I go back home to clean air and clean, available water. The Sisters and the poor live with it every day. It's a brutal city ... a tough place in a world full of great injustice.

God be merciful to all who cannot even afford a bowl of rice.

PAUL

When Paul was 16, he fell off a train at Howrah Station. He had been playing there with friends. Like many of the poor in India, he didn't go to school as his family couldn't afford it. Paul broke his neck and was paralyzed from the waist down. I was blessed to meet Paul and his family.

If the Sisters tell you that you are going a short way down the road for a visit, you can expect a five-mile walk. This particular five-mile walk with Sister Elizabeth and Ancellus took us to Paul's house.

I marveled at how the Sisters knew the way; Calcutta and the outskirts are like a maze and nothing is marked. If it is marked, the pollution usually hides the name, but we always arrived.

Paul never complained … he was never without a smile. I loved seeing him. Eight people lived in a small dark room. Paul's bed was on long poles; his four younger brothers slept underneath; his mother and sisters were next to them separated by an old plastic tarp.

Paul had deep bedsores; they develop on anyone lying in the same position for long periods of time. Three times a week, the sisters and I went to visit Paul. Each visit the Sisters brought rice and soap. Many days I would see by their small cooking stove dishes empty except for perhaps a few green beans. But still in spite of everything, there was peace and joy. Our arrival was usually announced before we arrived and everyone had on their best saris and smiles. Hope and happiness lived there.

Above Paul's bed was s picture of Jesus smiling, with one light bulb illuminating their humble abode.

One day as I was examining Paul, I noticed tiny bleeding shred marks on his feet. I knew but did not want to know—rats had been eating his toes and he could not feel it. I bought rat poison and was going to put it at the end of his bed. Sister told me that they would not eat the poison—once they had tasted flesh, they will not go to something else. I bought thick woolen socks. This would halt them for a time.

Paul's condition gradually improved. We taught his mother, brothers, and sisters how to care for him.

Our last visit was long and dusk was falling. We had a long way to walk. As we left, the lights went out, and Calcutta in the dark is scary. As we walked, we always prayed. The Sisters said to pray harder as we must be nearing the fork in the road ... if we miss it, we could get very lost.

The lights came on just as we approached our fork in the road.

When we turned, the lights went off again. The power of prayer.

Paul died in 1999. It was a sad day for every one of us who knew him. Sister Elizabeth told me that he died peacefully in his sleep and with a beautiful smile on his face.

Life in Calcutta.

"JOYA"

The fragrant flowers are called "joya." I've never seen or smelled a flower quite like "joya," and I believe they are only to be found in India. Slightly gardenia-scented ... tiny, beautiful white flowers.

A MOST KIND AND GENEROUS MAN

Consulate Generals who represent their countries are generally not like the German Consulate I met in Calcutta.

He was a rare person. He loved everyone, but he and his wife especially loved the Sisters and the street children of Calcutta, the orphans. They were all made welcome at the German Consulate.

There is a parable in the Bible that talks about the great feast and inviting the unloved, lonely, unwelcomed, the poor. This parable sums up the German Consulate.

Along with the Sisters and the children, I was also always invited. Each month he opened the grounds for all of us. He brought out the best foods, wonderful toys, puppet shows, a merry-go-round, new clothes (bought with his own money) for children in need. It was wonderful and spectacular. To this day, I've never seen a puppet show to compare to the two I saw there. Each child and adult was treated simply, yet in a grand style. The Sisters and their novices played volleyball. What great fun!

I remember the day that he was transferred back to Germany. It was a sad day for all.

Calcutta was never quite the same.

BUGS

I hate bugs, especially cockroaches. Spiders are right up there, too. Centipedes are probably number three, but let's move on. They are all alive and well and a good majority of them make their home in Calcutta.

On my first trip to India, I was naïve enough to think that surely God would not allow rats, cockroaches, or any other crawling beasts to be in Mother Teresa's presence. I was soon to learn differently.

I desired having a bb-gun when I saw this cockroach slowly ambling along a floor at the Shishu Bhavan. You couldn't step on it, but you could shoot it. You know where he went because his feet clicked on the floor. I learned that on my first trip. Some are so fast, they are gone when the lights come on. Others, like the big guys, move slower. They resemble the kids' battery-operated cars.

If you see a big spider there, leave it alone. If you see a little one, leave it alone, too. It's a no-win situation. I still have a scar on my inside left arm from a spider bite. That was my fifth trip. I like to think it was small, the spider, because if it was big, it's too much for my imagination.

I saw the biggest centipede ever in the room of the Mother House where the Sisters keep the bags of rice. I thought somebody had left a sandal there until it moved and scurried away on its hundred legs. I screamed really loud.

The Sister with me said, "It's just a bug."

Some things seem bigger than they really are.

THE CROWS

Next to bugs, I hate crows. They are aggressive, loud, big, and they take advantage of weakness. When I hear a crow or see one, my imagination takes me right back to Calcutta. Hearing a crow is like playing a movie for me. Not a good movie, a bad one ... the scene the same.

They bring me back to the huge garbage dump on the way to the new market by Sudder Street. Small children, adults sifting through the remains looking for food or something to burn to keep warm or even wear.

And the crows swooping down on the weakest, challenging them, and then taking things and flying off.

The Sisters found a baby near the garbage dump one day and brought her to the Shishu Bhavan. She had tiny rips by her eyes and mouth. I couldn't figure out what they were.

Sister Annette said, "The crows."

The Sisters found her in time, and she got better. I watched her tiny face heal.

SICKNESS

One year I got it all. It's very humbling to be sick.

Mother and the Sisters would say, "God has given you a gift."

My fifth trip to Calcutta, God gave me many gifts. Dysentery, worms, parasites, scabies, lice, and, oh yes, the spider bite. I was a mess. It was very hot and humid on this visit, and that added to my misery.

I learned to appreciate marble floors; they stay cool. On my worst day, I laid on the marble bathroom floor. My friends would stop in and chat, wipe me off, and bring me colas. They were wonderful, the colas. My friends who came by had the same plagues now and then. Their house calls were heaven. They knew what it was like.

Sister Andrea and Sister Shanta brought me a medicine mud ball from China. It was small but it worked. The medicine smelled really bad and I protested that I couldn't do it, but you don't argue with Sister Shanta. I took it, and within the hour, I was 99.9% better.

The greatest gift from the sickness?

Empathy ... for all of the suffering in India.

Seeing that my suffering is nothing compared to theirs.

Learning the true value of suffering in a city where suffering is a way of life.

THE MASHIS

Rupa was a mashi.

Mashis in India are hired for their skill to nurture or to be there for a person of means. Mother Teresa and the Sisters employ mashis. The mashis are incredible. They work hard all the time. They are paid, but it's very minimal. For Calcutta and India and the MCs, the mashis are essential. They cook, clean, and love. The MCs appreciate the mashis because it frees them to do more with the poor.

I want to bring them all home with me. Life would be fabulous.

Rupa loved the babies and the young children. She worked at the Shishu Bhavan. She always smiled. She loved her job. If I were holding or feeding a baby, she might say, "Auntie, do it this way." I figured I would do it Rupa's way—she had a degree in love.

The same mashis have been working with the MCs for years—caring, loving.

Perhaps their work may not seem like much to the world. Or a resumé.

But we know.

They worked for Mother Teresa.

"AUNTIE, AUNTIE!"

"Auntie, Auntie!" How many times in Calcutta I have been summoned by a call of "Auntie," most often at Kalighat or the Shishu Bhavan.

I didn't know what to think at first. But I grew to love being called "Auntie."

In India, "Auntie" is a kind term, a term of respect, a name used for you if you are a woman who is somewhat older than younger, a term of endearment. It is used by the Indian people, and only for women who are not Indian. If you are not Indian, you never call anyone "Auntie."

I was honored to be called "Auntie."

THE CITY OF JOY

It's a true place, "the City of Joy"—made famous by Dominique Lapierre, the French writer, and also by the film version of the book with Patrick Swayze in the lead role.

I read the book. I saw the movie. You still cannot believe it unless you see it.

The City of Joy is a separate part of Calcutta. To get there you have to take a boat across the Hooghly River. The boats are in very bad repair. I have looked into the water on the way across and prayed we would not sink. The water is pitch black ... from pollution. Occasionally I would see an arm or leg. Many Indians throw their loved ones in after death—they use it as a burial place.

Across the river at the end of the ride is the City of Joy. The MCs have a house there. I worked there one day, just to see it. It was unforgettable.

I remember standing outside on the roof of the house and looking out over the City, seeing the garbage piled up, mounds upon mounds everywhere, and the children on the street with bloated bellies, either from hunger or worms. Wall-to-wall people. They say that the City has the densest population of anywhere in the world.

More poverty, dirt, filth, pollution, disease, rats, living in the streets. It's worse than the worst of Calcutta. And yet, even in these extreme conditions, the people were smiling, peaceful—it *was* the "City of Joy." They were wealthy in the things that mattered.

I couldn't take a photograph. It would've been too invasive.

The City of Joy actors stayed at The Fairlawn Hotel on Sudder Street. That's where the British royalty always stayed. Many pictures adorn the lobby of this hotel, including one of the Queen of England and the Prince and Princess of Wales.

I read in a magazine interview that Patrick Swayze said working in Calcutta changed him. His eyes took in the poverty and all the injustices that poverty brings. His role was as a doctor who ends up defending the rickshaw drivers and their families. The movie did not come close to portraying the harsh reality of the physical and economic hardships of these men. But at least it tried.

I liked the movie. But there was one thing in it that really made me smile: Patrick Swayze always had on a fresh, clean white shirt.

My smile broke into laughter.

No one's shirt stays white in Calcutta.

THE BROKEN HIP

Sister Shanta was soft this day. It was the first time since I had known her that I saw tears.

An older man who had pulled a rickshaw all his life had an accident the previous week. While pulling the rickshaw, he stepped into a hole. As he fell on his side, he fractured the upper part of his hip. He got up and, for an entire week, he continued to pull the rickshaw. He had mouths to feed and he *had* to work.

The pain and swelling became so intense that he came to the Dispensary at the Shishu Bhavan. Sister Andrea made sure he had an x-ray. Sister Shanta and I took care of him.

We were all stunned at the x-ray picture. Working for a week after *this* injury? How had this man accomplished this?!

The pain alone would kill a young, strong man.

We were in awe of what he had done for a week just so his family would eat.

One father's response to the call … giving of himself, of love for his family.

JIM KNOWS

Jim is from Australia.

Jim left Australia to volunteer with Mother Teresa and the Sisters. He sold his home, his property, everything. He never went back to Australia again. His life is now in India.

Everyone knows Jim. If the Sisters or Brothers ever need help—Jim is always there. He gives of himself to the MCs and to the poor of Calcutta especially at Kalighat.

One evening, we were on the bus together going from Kalighat to the Mother House for Vespers, the evening prayer service. It was dusk. That's when the mosquitoes usually come out and feed. We humans are their evening meal. It can be miserable.

On this particular evening, Jim said to me, "You know, Katie, this represents life to me here. All this—the crowds, the chaos, the hardship all of it. I could never leave this now. This is life."

Jim knows ... it is life ... life lived to the fullest.

MOTHER'S CHRISTMAS TRADITION

Each Christmas, Mother Teresa wanted to have something special for the rickshaw pullers or "rickshaw wallas" as they are called. It's a term like bus drivers or streetcar operators: "rickshaw wallas."

Mother knew just how difficult life was for them. The rickshaw was their home. Their belongings were kept underneath the seat—this was it. And the work was extremely hard. And the pay? Well, bad. None of these men actually own the rickshaws. They are rented.

Each rickshaw walla had a bell—similar to a cowbell but with a sound like a "thunk" not a "ring-a-ling" ... like a car honking its horn at you. The rickshaw rang his bell, hoping you would ride with him.

Each year—and it continues—Mother and the Sisters bought as many blankets as they could and handed them out to the rickshaw wallas at Christmas. Those blankets were the best gift ever. I had great fun each time in India buying and bargaining for blankets, knowing the great and necessary and needed gift it would be throughout the years.

To this day, whenever I make a bed and fold a blanket, I think of the rickshaw walla that worked for a week with deathly pain just to feed his family.

And I wish I had a bigger suitcase to bring lots of blankets from home for the rickshaw wallas and Mother's Christmas Tradition.

ONE HUMAN FAMILY

[Excerpt from a 1999 letter from Sister Andrea, MC]

Calcutta this year has gone thru' hard times—we've had unusual rains and floods, right in the city as well as in the countryside (where it was worse!). Much of this year's harvest had been destroyed, but even the immediate hunger and distress of the people were grim. Our Sisters reached out daily to villages cut off completely from main roads. It was tragic to see little children holding out their hands from far for the cooked hot food—they had not eaten anything for 3, 4, even 5 days! Politicians of the world hold big conferences, make big agendas and promises, businessmen go on calculating their profits, and many others with fine houses and plenty of food can feast and dance away a fortune! When will we learn that we are ONE human family? All of us children of the ONE Father. We have still a long way to go....

But it is always a joy to see when there is spontaneous sharing—and a generous sharing. People who reach out to other people, totally unknown to each other—and doing so with a pure heart. The cry for help being the only reason to reach out, not name or fame. Then God himself fills them with that unique joy which comes from a sincere concern for a brother or sister in need. Let us thank God for the changes he gives us to keep that love and concern in our hearts. As someone once said—Perhaps the only reason for the state of helplessness is that it gives birth to compassion. What WOULD become of our hearts, if they had no more reason to reach out in self-forgetfulness? They could become hard like stone!

Kalighat—
Mother's Favorite

REALITY

Kalighat—Mother's hospital for the destitute and dying. In Hindu—Nirmal Hriday.

Mother Teresa loved Kalighat. It is said that Kalighat was her favorite, her "baby" ... the place where it all came together, where the ending of life came with a great deal of love.

I quickly grew to love Kalighat, too. It became, and still is my favorite. By "Kalighat," I mean the patients, the Sisters, the Brothers ... the love felt and shared. Every year I have gone to Calcutta, I have worked at Kalighat. During the first years, I worked there almost every day, throughout the day. I looked forward to spending my days there.

There is not a day that goes by that I don't think of Kalighat. It taught me so much. I became a hospice nurse back in the States because of my experiences there.

While I love Kalighat, in many ways it's a worst nightmare come true. People who have suffered all of their lives come there either to recover and have "another go at life" on the streets of Calcutta or go home in peace to God. The suffering and poverty of those who live on the streets, the often painful and protracted dying process, is incomprehensible.

I often think about the years of intense suffering the patients have endured, and the peace on their faces as they leave this world.

It makes me think they must achieve some of the highest places in heaven.

THE PARAKEET'S RESPONSE

The rhythm of life at Kalighat ... simple and peaceful, amidst the reality of death and dying.

Each morning, the day begins with prayer and a song. Then breakfast for the patients. Afterwards, dishes done by one team, then laundry started. A bit later, the men volunteers or Brothers give men baths, and the women volunteers or Sisters give women their daily care. Then medications are given, followed by wound care. After the noon to 3:00 p.m. rest, we would come back to work, ending the day with doing the dishes after the patients had their dinner.

As you enter Kalighat, the men's section is on the left, and the women's is on the right. In between the men and women's sections there were and still are always a number of birds—parakeets and others, like canaries. One year, there was this parakeet ...

That bird was a paradox.

As at hospice, so at Kalighat, not everyone dies. Some recover and are discharged to live again for a time. That parakeet knew. According to the patient's condition, he fully took on that patient's suffering or well-being.

At one point, there were two different patients beneath the parakeet. One did well and recovered, and the other suffered and died. When the patient who died suffered, the parakeet picked the majority of his feathers out. He hung his head. He looked awful. When the patient who lived thrived, the parakeet flourished. His feathers grew. He bounced around and was quite cheerful.

That was 1995, the year I remained in Calcutta two months, working every day at Kalighat. With each patient, the parakeet followed the same pattern—feathers or no feathers.

That parakeet always seemed to know.

THE ANTS

Now I want to remember the lady being eaten by the ants.

I learned much from this experience. Why would I even complain of one thing when this woman probably spent her whole life in abject misery, and then in the end, the ants were eating her ears. We had to put ant poison around the bed poles to keep them away.

Sister asked me to put an IV in so that near the end she would be more comfortable. So one day I gave her fluids and some bits of rice and yogurt. Her teeth were very rotten, and it was hard to get the food around them on her tongue so that she could swallow. Only Jesus knows what a weakness this was for me.

As I turned around to get ready and have the bed bath done, I could tell she would die. She died ten minutes later ... with all the Sisters, myself, and the German lady praying for her.

One ant came and began crawling on her face. I pinched him. He left this world before she did.

I felt very privileged to pick the last ant from her.

FATHER AND DAUGHTER

I noticed her right away.

Her head was shaved and she looked to be about five years old. I later learned she was seven. I first saw her sitting cross-legged on a small rug. It was Sunday at Kalighat, and Mass had just ended. The Sisters were busy, but I noticed that all of them would stop by the young girl and touch or pat her. She would smile. She was loved.

And then a man came and sat with her. His head was shaved. He gave her a dish of rice. They sat very close to each other. Yes, a resemblance. She had the eyes of her father.

The Sisters had found them both, father and daughter, lying in the street together. They were stricken, probably with malaria. To Kalighat they both went. At Kalighat, they were both prayed for and loved in their sickness. Daily they both got stronger.

Discharge day. I watched them walk out together ... father and daughter, hand in hand.

A most special success story.

"Thumbs Up"—Meena's Story

Meena was fifteen years old, and she was beautiful. Her family had promised her in marriage, but her dowry was not sufficient for the groom or his family. The marriage did not take place. The groom and his family did not want her, but they did not want anyone else to have her.

They threw acid on her from her neck down to her toes.

She had horribly infected burns and wounds. She was bandaged from her neck down to her toes with taped holes so she could go to the bathroom.

Her family did not want her. They took her to Sealdha Station and left her on the platform. The Sisters found her after she had lain there for several days. They brought her to Kalighat. Sister Luke and four of us volunteers would be involved in her care.

The bandages were filthy. I knew that there was great infection underneath them. They would need to come off and a catheter would have to be inserted. Sister Luke, the young woman from Sweden, Clare, Kim, and I smothered her with love; all of us just being in her presence, were touched by what she had endured at such a young age.

I was elected to insert the catheter. But before doing this, we asked Meena, "What would you like most of anything you could have?" Her answer, "A Thumbs Up Cola." Well, she could have had anything, but that's what she chose.

Meena had the most beautiful brown eyes and the most beautiful lovely dark black flowing hair. We combed her beautiful hair and tried as best we could to prepare her for the medical procedure. We all surrounded here while she drank the "Thumbs Up." She was so happy and we were delighted to be able to fill this simple request.

Meena was terrified of any more pain, but it had to be started. I went to prepare an injection, something to make her relax. Meena looked at all of us. Then she closed her eyes and died.

I believe her heart was broken and she could not take anymore. God called her home very quickly. For me, life stood still for a moment. We were all devastated.

We washed her and wrapped her tiny body in a shroud. None of us spoke, but we all cried and cried. We put beautiful flowers in her hair and placed many more flower blossoms upon the shroud. The Sisters held her body for two days hoping the family would come, but they never did.

I think of this child nearly every day since I met her. And every time I speak to Clare or Kim, we talk about "Thumbs Up" and what sweet pleasure that gave her.

And about the small things … done with great love.

ANDY LOVES THEM ALL

Everybody who's been to Calcutta knows Andy. His life has been spent helping and working alongside the Sisters.

Andy is a no-nonsense, take charge, get-it-done-kind-of-guy. And what a heart … big, soft, open. India and Calcutta captured Andy's heart.

Andy is from Germany. He's still a German citizen, but he sold everything and made Calcutta his home especially Kalighat. You cannot think of Andy without thinking of Kalighat. He is as much a part of Kalighat as the patients. The patients are Andy's people, his family—the unloved, the unwanted, and especially the children.

One year, a young boy had been brought to Kalighat with brain malaria and perhaps meningitis, a lethal combination. Narian had been found at Sealdha Station. He had been given up for dead more than once. Andy would hold him like a baby and talk with him about anything and everything, and I would feed him through a tube. He was in a coma. Not much hope.

One Sunday, during the Mass at Kalighat, we moved his cot; Narian would come to Mass, too. The MC brothers began the music and their beautiful singing.

Andy saw the flicker of the lids.

That Sunday was the beginning. Slowly, but surely, Narian's eyes opened. The next day, like a wobbly colt with help, Andy had him walking. We all held out our arms. Narian would walk to each of us and kiss us.

Narian's fifteen-year old body was very frail, but he was going to make it.

"And that kiss" ... Andy summed it up—the sweetest kiss we ever had.

THE UNKNOWN WOMAN

She would not say her name.

She spoke little. Her few words were only to thank. She never complained. She only smiled.

Every limb had a sore. Each finger was gnarled so her hands formed a cup. No one who passed by her bed at Kalighat failed to notice her frame. She was so thin. Her flesh was only a covering for her protruding bones.

I was privileged to care for her. Her cupped hands always reached out to caress me. She loved the green electro-light drink, but she could only take small sips. She was dying. I stayed with her.

Death would come soon.

She kept holding out her arms. They were pointed in the air with a beautiful look on her face. She appeared to be greeting someone or many people. I wondered what her life had been like. Did she have dreams as a young girl? Did she marry? Was she loved? Did she have children?

Her past was unknown.

But not the present.

She was reaching out to heaven, her true home, where she was not unknown.

JEN, JEREMIAH AND OUR GUY

Jen and Jeremiah aren't married or a couple. They are two young friends from Seattle.

I met this great young team at Kalighat. At the time, they were both nineteen years old. They were on a mission from the university.

Jen was an aspiring nurse. She already had great skills. She worked in a surgeon's office. She had seen, helped, and known medicine. The doctor she worked for had been instructing and training Jen one-on-one. He gave her street-smart skills—a great prep for Calcutta.

Jeremiah was a young man in his prime at school, reflective, a thinker. His heart became set on Indian adventure ... a calling? Only God knew for sure what was and is in store. The call for Jeremiah seemed strong, but a call to or for what? He would say, "For whatever." He will go gladly, willingly. He does not have a clue, but God does.

I'd been a nurse for many years—I was old enough to be their mother. And yet ... Jen and Jeremiah were experienced in ways I could not imagine. They were organized and ready. They mixed medications, prepared dressings, saw and understood problems, and mended them. At 19, they grew in ways far beyond their years. I was privileged to work along side them.

Before their first day was over at Kalighat, four or five hours at the most, the under-girding was set. Jen and Jeremiah were no longer students from the U.S. They were seasoned, ready for life—souls pounded like tender meat, softened.

Here was life in the raw. They had read about it. Now they were living it.

The three of us tended to a man who had an infected leg. It seemed that no matter what antibiotic we tried or packing we put in the wound, nothing was sufficient. It just got worse.

One of us gave "Our Guy" a pain injection. The wound care had become quite extensive. It took almost an hour. Even with the injection, Our Guy suffered. When we would remove the wound dressings from the prior change, a bowl had to be placed to catch all the pus that would run out. almost as if a faucet was on inside his leg. An Indian doctor came as a favor to the Sisters to see him. Still the infection got worse.

The three of us became very attached to Our Guy. As for him, when he saw us coming, he began saying many things. Hindi is a fast-spoken language. I knew what he was saying—it wasn't flattering.

Jeremiah always held his hand and spoke softly to him. It was always touching for me to see this. One day Our Guy was so weak. He said nothing to us in Hindi, but his eyes said everything. Jeremiah knew. Jen knew. I knew. Our Guy suffered terribly. When he died, I believe he went to one of those very special places in heaven.

Jen and Jeremiah? Their hearts were tenderized—a gift to all who came under their care.

They'll be back.

HARU

He was twelve years old. Bed #5 at Kalighat became his home.

Haru was found by the volunteers at Sealdah Station. He lived at Sealdah. He was left there by his family ... or separated. It was unclear.

Haru is in the lower caste system. Their belief is that if you endure the neglect and abuse, your next life may be better.

Haru did not speak.

His left foot was mangled in an accident at the train station. When he was finally found, the infection was great. The accident was the good out of the bad. Perhaps a lot of love and care at Kalighat could not only help to mend his young foot, but also try to help heal the pain and damage of abandonment, of missed love.

Everyone at Kalighat desired God's good for Haru. Love, care, food, hope, attention, healing. He began receiving all of it through the hands of the Sisters and the volunteers.

Haru is loved.

His present life was becoming better.

MIRACLES HAPPEN

A great gift this evening shift at Kalighat.

A young man, retarded, had been run over by a rickshaw driver. He had osteomyelitis. His lower leg bones from the mid-calf on down were like mush. He probably had been lying in the streets for a week or longer before he was brought to Kalighat. There was a very deep infection. His legs would probably need to be amputated.

I began caring for him about a week after he was brought in. And today, this young man's wound—a wound I did not see for a day and a half—has healed.

It was as if a set of hands had come during the night and carefully taken the bones and placed them together. We know that the healing is miraculous ... the course of healing should have taken months.

Sister Luke and Andy said that there are many such miracles at Kalighat.

It is true ... we saw them.

The power of prayer.

TAMAL'S DESIRE

Tamal was young, bright, and lived in Calcutta. He was exceptional.

Tamal was about sixteen or seventeen years old when I first met him at Kalighat. He was not a street kid. His family was not rich, but he went to school. He had a desire in his heart. He wanted to help. He was so eager to learn.

He came to Kalighat every day—every day—after school to volunteer his help. He wanted to learn more, and so Sister Luke had me teach him nursing skills … injections, preparing and mixing medicine. He learned quickly. He was a good student. And, he added "the Dispensary" to his schedule on Saturdays traveling with the medical team to the village. He went every week.

The last few times that I've been to Calcutta, I haven't seen Tamal.

I'm not sure where his path has taken him, but I know he is doing good somewhere.

THE JESUITS

A lady had been brought to Kalighat one night. She was probably fifty years old. She appeared much older. Her life had been hard.

The next morning she was being fed by a young Japanese girl. She was smiling. Maybe she felt safe for the first time in a long time. Then the change. It was fast. She probably had had a stroke. I was the only nurse at Kalighat that morning; I was on the men's side. A young girl came and said, "Hurry, come, someone is choking." When I got to her bedside, I knew she was dying. I started to get one of the Sisters to pray for her. Sister Terracina was coming and two men were with her.

I had seen the two men briefly over the prior few days. They had been walking and talking with each person. I didn't know they were priests. They were Jesuits from Goa, in the South of India. They wanted to come and serve at Kalighat. Sister Terracina knew, but none of the rest of us knew they were priests. They wanted it this way. They did not want to be spared anything.

We all surrounded the bedside as our lady was taking her dying breaths. The priests were so humble. They said, "Please, may we pray. We are priests." One of them began praying and blessing her. As the holy water was poured, I saw one tiny drop go in her mouth, and she was gone. Her face was radiant and she was smiling. It was so fast.

As we bathed her, I noticed her right arm. It probably had been broken but never set or mended. It was extended in an L-shape.

I'll never forget the humble Jesuits who only wanted to come and serve.

They were in the right place at the right time.

There are no accidents in God's plan.

THE LITTLE BOY AND HIS GRANDMOTHER

There once was a little boy who lived with his grandmother by Kalighat. The little boy's mother died when he was a year old. His father was gone most of the time. His grandmother loved him very much. He was six years old when he got very sick.

His grandmother took him to Kalighat. She needed the Sisters' help because she was afraid he would die. The Sisters helped the grand-mother and the little boy. He got better.

Sometimes the boy and his grandmother would come and sit inside Kalighat just to say hello and maybe have a meal. Leftover egg and rice or dal and the very tasty Indian sweets were given many times on Sun-days. The Sisters gave the little boy and his grandmother their own dishes so they could come and take food home or sit and eat.

One day the little boy came a little late and all the food seemed gone. He had such a sad face. He knew he and his grandmother might not eat that day.

We all saw the face. Before you knew it, leftovers came out!

The sad face ... well, it became a very happy one.

And so did all of ours.

THE HARP

I did not know her name, but she was elegant and had the most exquisite beauty. I'll never forget the gift she brought and gave to all of us.

The New York Philharmonic is famous. This elegant lady came from her orchestra across the ocean to Kalighat. She came to play the harp for the patients there. She had met Mother Teresa; soon she and the harp were in Calcutta. If you have traveled to India, you know this was not easy. I do not know the details, but she got there and I'll never forget it.

She arrived in the morning ... elegant and beautiful. She had on a long gown, and was perfectly coiffured; she looked regal. She and the harp played for hours. She never stopped.

It was heavenly. We all fell in love with the harp ... and with the elegant woman who came to share her gift with all of us.

THE SLAP

I love the Spanish people—they are so full of life, so exuberant.

One day in Calcutta, there was a group of about 50 people from Spain at the Mother House. On this particular day, Mother was surrounded by exuberant Spaniards.

I was leaving the Mother House after morning Mass. Mother liked to speak to each of us or touch us before we went off to work. But this day I did not wish to disturb her, so I went around the group and ended up ducking down by Mother to make my escape.

I felt a light, loving slap on my left temple. I knew it was Mother.

We all came to know "the slap." We welcomed it, waited for it.

Mother said, "Wait."

She always had time for us ... even when she had no time.

It's amazing how something so small—a light, loving slap—can mean so much ... and stay with you for a lifetime.

LETTER FROM TAMAL

November 1995

Dear Katie,

Hi! How are you? I hope everything is wonderful with you and your family. You must be wondering how I did get your address. The Holy Spirit gave it to me!!! How is your mother now?

When are you coming back to Calcutta? Here everyone is doing quite well. I do give injections regularly (with good confidence). Thank you so much. The full credit goes to you. You were such a nice and patient teacher. And you know!!! A few days ago Sister Luke told me to help the newly-professed Sisters to learn to give injections. I was fascinated with the trust she has in my skills. The first thought that came into my mind then was about you.

Thank you, Katie, for everything that you shared with us. May God bless you always. Whenever you remember us, please pray for us. You are always in the hearts and prayers of your friends here.

With love,
Tamal

Silent Saints

WHO ARE THEY?

If I wrote about everyone I've met or everything I've seen in Calcutta, the book would be too big to print. But there's one thing I have to write about ...

While working with Mother and the MCs over the years, I have had the gift of meeting people from all over the world—volunteers so committed and so giving. Often they did not know the effect they were having on others or on me.

I call them "silent saints."

Andy. Jen and Jeremiah. Jim. Noel. Pedro. Clare and Kim. Mattius. Tamal. Jorge. The list goes on. They are men and women from all walks of life—wealthy and of lesser means, famous and hidden, old and young, quiet and bold, educated and simple, cultured and naïve, strong and broken. Yet they all had one thing in common: a love for the MCs and the poor of Calcutta, a love that manifested itself in action.

I was privileged to know these remarkable souls. Many are my friends to this day.

They all helped to spread the fragrance.

"HARRY, DON'T BE LATE!"

There's one more thing about Harry ...

"Harry, don't be late." These are words I ended up speaking frequently to Harry.

Harry never missed a need. Each person was special. Each need was met. If someone was lying on the side of the road, Harry always stopped "just to make sure they were okay." It may have been their street home in Calcutta, but Harry always needed to know.

And so, Harry was always late.

Harry's doctor skills never were wasted in Calcutta, and Harry was always happy, full of energy. And he always saw the best in everybody and every situation. He made me crazy. But he taught me a lot. As a doctor and nurse, we were a great team.

One night before we left Calcutta for our homes in the States, I said, "Harry, don't be late; we will miss the plane. The cab will be here at 5:00 a.m." Harry replied, "I'll see you. And I won't be late!"

Was Harry late? 5:00, 5:15, 5:30 ... I knew there was a need somewhere. I took the cab. The plane boarded at 7:00 a.m.

Harry? He made the flight just as the doors were closing.

He was late, but the need was met.

Thank you, Harry, for showing me that being on time is not always the most important thing.

ESTHER'S EXCESS LOVE

Esther's husband died. She loved him very much. She had so much left-over love.

Esther's excess love needed to be spent and given.

I met Esther at Kalighat on my first trip to Calcutta. As a spoiled American nurse, I did not really know the procedure for cleaning and re-using the disposable rubber gloves. Esther taught me this with great love. Esther also taught me how to put grief into action with her service to God.

Now, Mother Teresa never cared about degrees, but she cared about doing small things with great love. Before Esther taught me how to clean the gloves, I watched her. I was a novice at so much, but it fascinated me to watch her disinfect the used gloves, discard the ones with holes, then rinse and dry and powder the others, and return them to the metal cans to re-use. Such a small, but a huge task.

Do I toss my gloves lightly at the hospital? Sometimes.

But I more often think of Esther.

And I remember how she put her love into action.

LEARNING FROM TANIA

When Tania was 16, she began working in the soup kitchen with the Sisters in London.

Tania loved working with the Sisters in London. She began going there every day after school—hard work, not easy for a young girl.

Then she took a job on Saturdays and began saving her money so she could go to Calcutta to work with Mother Teresa. Three years later and nearly 20, she arrived in Calcutta in 1997. She would stay for one year. My daughter, Linda, and I were privileged to know her.

She accepted each and every situation and person. She had a gentle soul and a soft touch. She especially loved feeding the ladies at Kalighat that were too weak to sit up. Tania would sit by them with dal and rice or whatever was for them easiest to eat. No matter how long it took, it was done. Slowly, bit by bit, the weakest recovered enough to sit up and eat by themselves.

When the patients would see Tania coming with breakfast or lunch, they always smiled and waved. And she went on to patiently and lovingly feed the newest patients.

Although young in age, Tania was mature beyond her years.

We all learned a lot from Tania.

FABIO—A CHANGED YOUNG MAN

Fabio left for Italy yesterday. He was a very special young man, not only because he was a handsome Italian, but he had been at Kalighat for two years. And for a young man to give up such a big chunk of his life, that's indeed rare.

At Kalighat, Fabio bathed, fed, and cared for the men. He never shied away from doing anything. He had such a presence. Now, he returns to Italy to go to school for one year.

Fabio told me that two years ago, when he came to Calcutta, he was a completely different young man—spoiled and selfish. He insinuated that his family, especially his father, were fed up with him, that he had done some "not so good" things back in Italy. I'm not sure what Fabio did before, but I do know what he did in Calcutta.

I do not think that his family will be distressed at the change.

It is always life-changing in India.

I wish our American court system could send offenders to work for the MCs in India.

I think it would eliminate a lot of delinquent and adult behavior problems.

CLARE'S SMILE

A smile is a gift, and you can return the gift or it can stop with you.

I "heard" Clare before I saw her. I heard the smile, the voice, the kindness behind a curtain. Ears don't always need eyes. So, blindly I "heard" Clare, and I thought. this is Kalighat. And while I know the joy and sweetness of God, it was Clare behind a curtain that captured this for me.

Clare captured the joy and love of giving.

Clare is from Georgia—a teacher, a woman of God, "on fire" in her faith, Southern Baptist. Instead of writing about Clare, I wish I could introduce the world to her. And then be like her.

Clare always smiles.

Some people smile and you know that beneath that lovely smile, the path leading to and from the heart is full of God's love. Clare's gift is joy. When Clare smiles, she doesn't just radiate, she glows. And it's so beautiful. She affects your day. It's better because of her smile, her gentle ways.

Clare lovingly washed the thin, broken bodies of the ladies at Kalighat each day. Nothing seemed to stop her smiling. Amidst death, sadness, and tremendous sorrow every day at Kalighat, the smile was always there and given so easily and willingly.

I remember a time when Clare was not well. She was literally a lovely pale green. And she was still smiling. If she suffered, only God knew it. Clare only smiled. She never complained.

I want to be more like Clare.

PIKWAH'S GRIEF

I never knew what happened to Pikwah after Calcutta.

But I know what happened to Pikwah before Calcutta and in Calcutta.

Pikwah was from Hong Kong. She was a new bride. Her name in Chinese means "green flower." Her honeymoon was going to be finished in India. She and her husband had already traveled together in Thailand and other areas of Asia. Her young husband traveled ahead a few days to prepare for their finale in India.

On his first day in India, he was crossing a busy street and a fast-moving car struck him. He died instantly. Pikwah told me of not hearing from him for two days and then receiving the news. She remembered nothing the first month afterwards. She was paralyzed with grief. She told me of her great love for her young husband and their plans to begin their lives together. Pikwah decided she would continue and finish the honeymoon.

She would go to Calcutta.

And spend her love and heartache caring for the unwanted and the dying.

Pikwah worked at Kalighat. She was loving, kind, and compassionate. She became God's hands. She was never tired; she walked everywhere. She would say to me, "Hi, hi, Katie, come let us walk together." She knew Calcutta well. She was using her grief for others.

One day she said to me, "My heart is still crushed. I don't know if I shall ever heal." I knew she would, but I also knew it would take a long time.

I know Pikwah has healed. The process in Calcutta was touching. I saw it.

I watched grief turn into pure love.

THE PRINCESS

One day I was speaking to Mother Teresa. She asked me if, when I returned home, I would be going through Asia. I said, "No Mother, I'll be going to London first. I have some friends there."

She said to me: "You know the Princess is there. We are friends. You should stop in and say hello."

She meant it. Nobody was exempt. Mother Teresa put everyone together. Nobody was more important than another.

I envisioned myself going to Buckingham Palace to give Princess Diana regards from India.

I never did.

But I still sometimes dream … about the tea I might have had in London with Mother's friend, "the Princess."

Titagarh—
The Abode of Love

A HOME OF RESPECT

The MC Brothers not only have a special place in my heart, they have a piece of it.

No, make that two.

One for the Brothers at Kalighat, and another for the Brothers at the Gandhiji Prem Niwas—"the abode of love," the leper colony founded by Mother Teresa at Titagarh.

Titagarh is located outside Calcutta … it's about an hour-and-a-half train ride from the heart of the city. It is one of the MC Brothers' many special ministries. The Brothers "manage" Titagarh. They help to provide a safe home and a sanctuary for the lepers, and it's all self-supported. The lepers do all the work. It's very impressive—a fish pond, gardens with vegetables, livestock, rooms with huge weaving looms … truly a self-sufficient community, nothing wasted, all utilized for the good of all who live there. They even have a hospital for needed surgeries.

Leprosy in India today is not uncommon. And lepers today, just as in biblical times, are separated and shunned. Titagarh is a safe haven. No one is turned away. Leprosy is treatable. Early stages can be halted with antibiotics. It must, however, be continued for life. The bacteria can be dormant and surface years later. This is rare, but it can happen.

Titagarh has visitors every day. Many people outside of India have never seen a leper or been to a leper colony. The MC Brothers always ensure during these visits that the residents are treated with respect, that their privacy is given due regard. They help to maintain their integrity.

I visited Titagarh the first time I went to India and on every trip afterwards. I brought medicine, bandages, vitamins, needles, and other supplies to the Brothers for the residents. And I always brought gifts from others including monies for their needs.

It is always a gift for me to be able to offer a little something for these exceptional people.

BROTHER VINOD ... AND THE PIGS

On my first visit to Titagarh, I met Brother Vinod. He was in charge of Titagarh. We became good friends and have remained so to this day.

A few years back he was assigned as the head of Minapour which was then a new leper colony about four hours from Calcutta. His experience at Titagarh was invaluable.

I still see Brother Vinod on almost every trip. His work often brings him to Calcutta for meetings and other needs for his community.

Brother Vinod is the epitome of the elegance of the Indian people. He is very private, very dedicated to God and the lepers, and very kind.

It was also Brother Vinod who introduced me to the pigs on my first visit to Titagarh. To this day, when I see a pig, I have to compare it to the pigs I saw at Titagarh.

These pigs were huge—very impressive, a bacon lover's dream come true. Happy pigs, too! They were *massive* and well-fed with leftovers. They even looked as though they were smiling.

Every time I see my friend, Brother Vinod, I inquire about many things, but I am always sure to ask, "Are the pigs getting bigger?"

I like seeing Brother Vinod smile.

THE LOOMS

In Titagarh there is a very large area with huge, huge looms. The looms at the leper colony operate continually.

The lepers weave all the cloth for the Missionaries of Charity communities around the world including all of the Sisters' habits. Nowhere else in the world is this cloth woven. Only at Titagarh.

The lepers also weave cloth to sell. The cloth is colorful, sturdy, and beautiful.

I'm fascinated by the looms. They are wooden. The loom rooms are long and large. All the patients and inhabitants take part here. It's amazing, the production of the beautiful sturdy cloth. You can purchase whatever you like—except the special colors and looms on which the Sisters' habits are woven.

When my daughter, Linda, came with me to Calcutta, I brought her to Titagarh. I bought some colorful pink and green checked colors, and solid green colors. And the Indian tailor made some wonderful shirts for both Linda and me.

My other tailor-made clothes eventually fell apart.

But my beautifully-woven Indian cottons are still intact.

CHRISTIE ANN'S DREAM

When she was four years old, she knew she wanted to care for the lepers in India. There was no doubt, no hesitation. This was her calling. she knew it.

It took 56 years for Christie Ann to realize her calling. The road to Calcutta had many bumps and roadblocks, but they served an important purpose; she was being prepared.

From Belgium to Calcutta. Finally, a few years ago, the doors swung wide open.

At the age of four, Christie Ann was told that she was a descendant of Father Damien of Molokai. Father Damien is on his way to becoming a canonized saint. He was a very holy priest who left everything in Belgium to live amongst and care for the lepers in Hawaii. Father Damien had a long preparation with many bumps and roadblocks. In the end, he also became a leper, shunned and separated from society. He died serving the people he loved.

I met Christie Ann in Calcutta. She came to begin what God had intended for her all along ... but still, a few roadblocks.

Christie Ann told the Sisters how she wanted to serve God and work directly with the lepers for the rest of her days on earth. She told them she wanted to work at Titagarh. The Sisters instead told her to first work with the handicapped children at the Shishu Bhavan. She did this—lovingly and willingly ... massaging, holding, serving. The children loved her. They knew her touch.

Then one day, Christie Ann was asked to please come and serve at Minapour. Oh, the happiness, the joy each day serving the lepers becoming God's hands for the shunned, the outcasts!

Kolkata
29th Sept. 2001

Dear Sister Katie,
These few lines I write to express our heartfelt sorrow and anguish over the death of so many innocent people of America. It is unbelievable that human beings could do such a horrific and heinous crime! No trace of thousands of people, Lord what a pathetic way to die!! Hatred is the greatest evil of this generation. Religion simply becoming an opium, it is used to divide and destroy each other. Communal harmony is lost forever. Here in India the fear of war looms large. The moment if war begins in Afghanistan there will be enough and more trouble in India also. Every day so many are gunned down by the terrorists in different parts of India specially in Kashmir.

People have started turning towards God, we could see people praying in temples, in mosques and churches for peace in the world. May the Prince of Peace have mercy on us all. Once again we brothers express our deep felt sorrow and pain at the loss of so many innocent American people.

United in prayer, Your brother in Jesus,
Br. Vinod, MC

Dear Sister Katie,

"Prayerful greetings." Thank you so much for the photos and small note, it reached me safely. Sisters from Mother House send it for me. I am extremely glad to hear that you have already arranged eye sutures for us. You are so prompt. Many a people promise us many a things, but few people really care. Just the other day I received two vital parts for our German microscope which was out of order for the last two years. It cost a lot for that family who took the trouble to search for it in Germany. Our eye surgeon will be glad. He gives his voluntary service for our patients every Saturday. Five to six operations he does every week. All for the Love of Mother and the poor! You have seen the plight of the poor in this part of the world. Hope you will continue to help us to help the poor, specially the leprosy patients. Next time when you come to India please spend some time with us, you could assist our Doctors in the O.T. A couple in Australia has sent a lot of surgical instruments for our new operation theatre. Very many good people all over the world!

Thank you sister once again for your love and concern. As I receive the material I will inform you. Assure you of my prayers. God bless.

Yours sincerely,
Bro. Vinod

Some Memorable Moments

THERE ARE NO ACCIDENTS

Noel lives in Sonoma only forty-five minutes from my home in California. I did not know Noel in California. I met her in Calcutta.

Five-thirty a.m. comes around early. Time for prayer and then Mass at the Mother House. I was crossing the street on my way to join the Sisters for the beginning of the day. A soft rain was falling. and the dust in the air and on the street was turning to mud.

I did not notice the dog that jumped at my back, but the lady walking behind me did. He was looking for food and, in his search, left some pretty distinctive paw marks.

We hurried to the convent. The quick clean up of my clothes before Mass revealed where we were both from. Another gift—a new friend to visit at home and spend time with in Calcutta.

I just then noticed a bandage on Noel's foot. She casually said, "Oh, I just stepped on a nail two days ago." I asked, "Did you get a tetanus shot?" She had not. The next day was the last day for a tetanus shot to ward off what would have been the inevitable lockjaw.

We went to the Dispensary. Sr. Andrea gave Noel the shot.

Noel is fine. We became and continue to be very good friends.

And the dog that jumped on me?

He probably saved Noel's life.

THE DENTIST

Somebody once asked me if I was afraid of flying or travel or whether I was ever just afraid.

Not really. When my time comes, it will come. Why worry or be anxious? God has numbered each one of the hairs on our heads.

But I must confess that I am afraid of something. Dentists.

I hate going to the dentist. It is a left-over fear from childhood when dentistry was more brutal. No Novocain, no gas. Pure pain.

Mother Teresa had a good friend, a dentist, with a practice in the City of Joy. One day, Sister Marcellina and I got into one of Mother's ambulances and took four children from the Shishu Bhavan for some dental work.

When we arrived, it took a lot of courage for me to smile—for the children's sake—rather than *run*. His office was an open doorway with an open sewer running in front of it. The floor was dirt. The roof was woven from palm fronds. He was a chain smoker; he had a cigarette going the whole time he worked, with a long ash that never seemed to fall off the end. That ash scared me—I can still see it.

But that wasn't all. Just then, the old-fashioned hypodermic needle came out.

Now, I was really scared. It was like an old horror movie.

I think my eyes may have gotten very big, but the smile stayed on my face. For the children.

I made a resolution then and there. Each time before I go to Calcutta, I go to the dentist.

I don't want to have any problems in Calcutta.

A SPECIAL AWARD

On one trip to India, the MC Brothers invited me to their main home outside of Calcutta. One of the Brothers I worked with at Kalighat wanted me to see a little more of their way of life.

It turns out that Mother Teresa was coming, too. The Brothers were giving her an award. To this day, I'm still not sure what the award was for, but I wouldn't have missed it for the world.

I got on a bus with the Brothers and others that had been invited. One of the MC Sisters who came was from Mauritius, an island off the coast of Africa. Her parents were with her. Her father was the Prime Minister. They were lovely. I was always amazed to meet so many MCs who came from well-to-do families. They were attracted by the simplicity and poverty of the life. So different from the way they were raised.

The bus ride was spectacular, although very bumpy. No paved roads on this trip. It was about an hour-and-a-half trip through the lush jungle. Palm trees, monkeys, exotic birds … every color imaginable. So much beauty such a short distance from so much poverty.

We arrived and the ceremony soon began. Afterwards, one of the Brothers came up to me and asked me if I wanted a photograph of Mother receiving the award. I told him that I did, and he gave it to me right then. He told me that I was only one of three people who have this photograph. I was humbled and felt very blessed.

It was dusk before we started on our way home.

I don't remember too much of the ride back.

I think I was still in awe of the entire day.

"KOLKATA"

I first learned the news when Sister Andrea wrote me during the Puja Holidays in 1999. The Indian government decided to make some changes; to recognize that Hindu was the country's official language. As a result, Calcutta became "Kolkata," the official spelling of the city in Hindu. And so with Bombay—which is now "Mumbi."

Whether it's spelled Calcutta or Kolkata, it still is my favorite city in India.

THE DIGNITARIES

During the mornings and evenings when we were at the Mother House, many important people from all parts of the world came to see Mother Teresa. I saw entourages of well-dressed men fall apart in her presence. I saw many dignitaries moved to tears. I saw many others bow down and grab onto Mother's feet—they wanted her blessing.

All of these men knew. God's presence surrounded this tiny woman. It was palpable.

Mother was very humble. She never sought fame or honor.

She always complied with their requests.

NOVEMBER 18

Friends make birthdays in Calcutta very memorable.

One year, we all decided to have dinner together. At Halem Galim Street, by the apartment I rented that year, there was an outdoor cooking stand. The owner of a small café cooked heavenly rice there. An open flame and a huge old metal pot—this cooks up the most incredible, tasty dishes. Vegetarian, rice or with some egg … this was the menu of the day and my birthday meal.

Another year we celebrated at Kalighat. So happy and so special. Dear Anna and Maruxa, my friends from Spain, sang me a song they wrote especially for me. Clare—a queen of beauties—got me a cake. Tamal, my dear Indian friend, put beautiful fragrant flowers in my hair and around my neck. Many friends signed and gave me a very special card.

And one year, my god-daughter, Sunita, gave me card.

I still have all of the cards.

Each day was so very, very blessed and lovely.

May God bless each person who made my birthday such a wonderful day for me.

THANK YOU

I have had an unmanageable fear. I hate speaking in public. One to one is okay, two is acceptable, but three or more is a crowd.

One year, on a Saturday, I was asked at the Mother House to read at Mass the next day, on Sunday. It was a short scripture reading. "Okay ... well, sorry but I can't ... I think I'm getting a cold." "That's okay, you will be fine tomorrow." Wrong excuse.

On Sunday morning, the Mother House chapel was packed, brimming over with visitors, dignitaries, and all the Sisters and novices. People were everywhere—on the landing and on the staircase ... an unusual amount on this Sunday. I could not concentrate on anything except my fear. Just what was that fear? I did not even remember how it became to have so much power over my life. It clutched my throat like an invisible hand. I trembled. As I passed Mother Teresa on my way to the podium, she glanced at me for a moment. She saw my fear.

I stepped two steps up to the small podium. I almost fainted as I felt the room swaying—my own personal earthquake. I read. I was scared and nervous. It showed. I stepped down after the reading, knowing just how awful I sounded. I was humiliated. My phobia had won.

I stayed on in Calcutta for another month and spent Christmas there. On Christmas Day, I was told by the Mass Coordinator that I would have a reading that day—Mother Teresa had specifically asked for me to read the second reading at Mass before the Gospel. After my first failure, I knew that Mother and the Sisters were praying for me.

Mass began. The place was packed again, overflowing. I walked by Mother Teresa. She looked at me and smiled. She remembered, and I remembered. I walked without fear or trembling. I was a little nervous, but no blurred vision. The reading was short, and I even looked at the people as I read. It went well. Except for the little bench that the reader stands on … I almost fell off when I was done because I was so ecstatic. I smiled as I walked by Mother Teresa. Her head was down in thoughtful prayer.

Mass was over. I got up to leave, and Mother Teresa was waiting for me by the entrance. She was beaming. It was Christmas and she had a line of dignitaries and visitors from all over the world, and she was waiting for me. She took my hands and said, "*Thank you.*"

Mother knew that a prayer had been answered. She remembered the first time, and she knew that when you do something again, whatever it may be, you have the opportunity to do it better.

She wanted me to grow.

Thank you, Mother.

MOTHER'S WORDS

Each time I have been in India, I have never gotten over the wonder of being in Mother Teresa's presence. Some days we would just have simple conversations, but they were always profound. I always came away wiser. Mother Teresa always got right to the point; she never wasted a word.

Simple, direct, easily understood, speeding directly to the soul—only what you need.

Mother Teresa's words never needed to be pruned.

THOSE HANDS

Mother's hands are the softest hands I have ever felt. I call them "bunny hands." It's like two soft bunnies caressing you.

Love and God's mercy and healing accompany her touch.

In her touch, life's pain leaves and healing occurs. When she touches you, God touches you.

You leave her presence truly touched by God.

The Shishu Bhavan— Caring for the Little Ones

EACH LIFE IS PRECIOUS

Mother Teresa said that the child is the beauty of God, the greatest gift to the family.

Mother sent the word out, "Please do not destroy the child; we will take the child." And she and the Sisters did. Mother founded homes for children throughout India: Shishu Bhavans. Calcutta's Shishu Bhavan was her first.

Thousands of boys and girls from throughout India have lived in these homes. All of them valued for the precious life they are. Mother and the Sisters have never turned a single child away.

Each Shishu Bhavan is a shelter, an orphanage, a haven for infants and children. The Sisters welcome each child; loving and caring for those that are abandoned as well as children brought to the Sisters by their families who seek help in caring for them. The children can stay for as long as needed—one day or several years.

Many of the children who have lived at the Shishu Bhavans have been adopted. Others have stayed well past their teens. Mother Teresa and the Sisters have been "mothers" to many over the years providing for each of them and their needs. Every child is loved, educated, and taught skills—so that one day they can leave and go out into the world. And when they marry, the Sisters participate with them in the ceremonies and customs of India and even provide small dowries according to Indian custom.

A few years back, in 1994, one of the young men left Calcutta's Shishu Bhavan and made his way in the world. He returned that year and asked Mother Teresa for a special girl's hand in marriage; she had remained at the Shishu Bhavan. Many of the children who live at the

Shishu Bhavans have grown up together. They have known each other all their lives.

The young woman said yes. Mother said yes. And the dowry was given.

A great event was about to happen—an Indian wedding!

THE WEDDING AND THE ENGAGEMENT

There is nothing like a wedding; but nothing can compare to an Indian wedding—except maybe the engagement.

I was invited to the wedding. Two of Mother Teresa's "children," two orphans who had known each other at the Shishu Bhavan, were going to be married! It was amazing; it was an event. I did not want to miss any of the excitement; it was tremendous. We were all like little kids.

On each day of the several days before an Indian wedding, there is a "happening." There are Indian customs—dinners, lunches, snacks, meetings, clothes picked, foods prepared.

And, oh yes, almost as big as the wedding is the engagement.

When I went to the engagement party, you would think that the couple had gotten married. It was that big of a day. I was exhausted. I can imagine how they felt.

First, all the invited women got together. It's a tradition to mix spices, especially turmeric, and take your fingers and smear some on the bride-to-be's face and each other's faces. The Indian women are beautiful and elegant even with these colors on their faces.

Then, the women and men and all of the invited guests came together. Indian sweets were shared. The priest held the couple's hands together and blessed the rings, and then blessed the couple and all of us. Then a very touching final scene ... the bride touched the feet of her soon-to-be husband. In India, the greatest sign of respect is to touch another's feet. It's a way of saying, "I honor you above others; in my eyes, you are it." I never forgot the touching of the feet. It was extremely powerful. All of us laughed and cried. It was a wonderful day.

When the wedding day came, we were all in our "best." Everyone looked gorgeous. I still remember every detail of my own attire—black and gold silk with pearls; it was elegant. The Indian women have a particular grace; they wear their saris like queens wear crowns. It's a gift just to watch the movements—the colors, the grace.

The bride was beautiful, shy, so loved. I will always remember the ceremony at St. Theresa's and the reception at the Shishu Bhavan.

A happy ending ... and beginning ... to two life stories.

MIRACLE OF THE SHELL

Today I woke up missing the ocean and Bodega Bay so very much. I was lying in bed telling this to Jesus. I was a bit homesick.

Also today, instead of working at Kalighat, I was to teach novices upstairs at the Shishu Bhavan for Sister Andrea. The novices learned blood pressure, IV's, IM's, medicines, subcutaneous injections, and different lung sounds. It was a good day.

So, as only God can do—as I was leaving the Shishu Bhavan, Sister Shanta said to me, "Here is your payment for teaching us this day."

Sister Shanta presented me with a beautiful, huge seashell so I could hear the sea.

I not only had the pleasure of teaching the dear Sisters who are so eager to learn, but Jesus was saying, "Yes, I heard you. You cannot have the sea, but you may have the shell I made so you can hear the beautiful sound you miss."

It was a good day for the Sisters.

And they also made it a special day for me.

BROTHER AND SISTER

A young brother and sister were brought to the Shishu Bhavan when they were two and four years old. Their mom and dad could not afford to feed them anymore. They suffered from tuberculosis.

After a few months, the children were brought back to their cribs, close to each other. They had been separated for their treatments for TB and various other ailments.

As young as she was, the sister never forgot her brother. When they were brought back close to each other again, she would go to him and feed him his bottle. Nobody else was allowed. Only her.

Their bond was never broken.

Brother and sister.

THE BATH

He seemed to have a permanent station by the Shishu Bhavan.

He was a child of the streets, probably nine or ten years old, and quite thin. He looked like he should be very fragile, but that thin little body had so much energy.

And he was very smart. His English was flawless, his Spanish quite good, French not bad. When he saw me some days, he ran along side saying the same thing over and over, "Please Auntie, Auntie, milk, biscuits." The gesture ... finger to the stomach, fingers to the lips, FEED ME. He was remarkable.

In the morning, the Sisters always fed him. The rest of the day it was whoever could. I never saw him standing still; he *was* constant motion. He had a thick head of beautiful black hair, but it was gray from dust and pollution. His thin body was streaked with mud. He needed a good bath.

One day in the afternoon, I didn't see him. I came into the Shishu Bhavan after the end of the afternoon rest. On the bench by the gate was my energy boy. He had had a bath; he was asleep on a bench; he was smiling. He was still.

A bath ... something so simple for us was a small bit of heaven for him.

ALBA AND THE TWINS

Alba was from Colombia but lived most of her adult life in Washington, D.C. Alba wanted to be a nun, but her family was against it. Alba accepted this and decided to serve God by working with the MC Sisters in Washington. If Alba was ever disappointed with her family's decision for her life, she never showed it. She accepted everything and became God's servant.

Alba came to India. She had met Mother Teresa in D.C. and wanted to experience Calcutta.

Alba is another silent saint.

Alba worked with the babies. This particular year, sets of twins came to the Shishu Bhavan—six sets. Two sets of the twins stayed at the Shishu Bhavan. They were identical; we could only tell them apart by their tags. Alba knew them the best. One twin ate slowly; the other twin gulped and the food was gone.

We found out that some days, the families could afford to feed one twin but maybe not both. The faster twin figured this awful event out at an early age. Alba, with her loving care, figured this out before the family told us this sad story of little food and double the mouths to feed.

So instead of name tags to identify our twins, whoever ate the fastest was "#1 twin" and our slow eater was "#2 twin." It took time, but soon both little girls under Alba's tender loving care ate at the same pace.

In the year of the twins, we all learned to hold a baby tucked under each arm.

And Alba taught us how some things become clearer with slow, loving patience.

THE MEASLES AND BANDEL

Many of the children in the orphanages at the Shishu Bhavan are very weak.

Some of them were born to mothers who themselves were severely malnourished, and after periods of no food or fluids, they are weaker still. Then they are brought to the Sisters—sometimes when they are on the brink of death.

When I was in Calcutta in 1994, an outbreak of measles occurred. It spread like wildfire among the children. They all were very sick, some worse than others. It was not good.

One night at prayer time, the Sisters prayed specifically that the outbreak would stop and that all the children would recover. The Sisters promised God a pilgrimage to Bandel in thanksgiving for this favor.

Bandel is a holy place dedicated to the Blessed Virgin Mary by the Portuguese and Indians. A miracle occurred there in the 1500's. A ship owned by the Portuguese, whose bow had been carved in an image of the Blessed Virgin, had been entrusted to her. As the story goes, the ship sank during a storm and for many years, no one knew its whereabouts. One day the villagers at Bandel began noticing a light at night off the coast; one of the villagers had a dream. In the dream, the Blessed Mother told the villager where she was; the light they were seeing was the carved bow of the ship. Our Lady was rescued and put in the church at Bandel. Since that time, many miracles have occurred there.

The next day at the Shishu Bhavan, the outbreak of measles stopped. Everyone recovered. Plans were immediately made to travel to Bandel, a two-and-a-half hour ride from Calcutta.

I was invited on the pilgrimage. We loaded the truck with all the children. Material had been donated, and every girl and boy had a new outfit to wear for the trip. The material was bright, hot pink. Everyone was wearing the same color. They were easy to spot.

What a wonderful day! Prayer, thanksgiving, food, fun, a lot of laughter.

The ride on the way home was just as joyful, but about half the way home, everyone had to go to the bathroom. So we stopped the truck in the dark. It was pitch black. We were in the middle of the pepper fields. All of a sudden, millions of fireflies came to life and the whole field lit up; mini-night lights … just what was needed for this part of the journey.

I'll never forget that day or that evening.

Sparkling night lights in a day and night of many miracles.

OH YE OF LITTLE FAITH

Sister Andrea always says, "Whatever talent or gift you bring to Calcutta, God will replace when you depart."

I was at the Shishu Bhavan in 1995 or 1996 taking care of a six-year old Indian girl who had been badly burned. Her wounds and burns took me a long time to dress—an hour-and-a-half in the morning and an hour-and-a-half in the evening. It had to be done slowly and with much care because of the pain and the normal behavior of young children.

The Sisters were always busy, so this task freed them up considerably. I had been doing this for two months, but I was leaving in three days. Sister Andrea said, "Katie, God knows we will need a replacement for you."

That afternoon, a young German man knocked on the Shishu Bhavan gate. "Sister, my name is Stephen. I am a medical student wanting to help. I'll be here for three months."

I know that when it was time for Stephen to leave, God brought his replacement.

SUNITA—MY SPECIAL CHILD

Sunita is a young lady now. She is in her twenties and very beautiful.

Sunita's hand has been asked for in marriage two times already. Sister Marjorie, who became head of the Shishu Bhavan after Sister Marcellina went to work in Goa, told me this, and she said that Sunita was not yet ready for marriage—the right suitor has not come yet.

Sunita is very shy. I took care of her when she was ten years old. Sunita's mother had died when she was six years old. She had seven brothers and her father.

The Sisters found Sunita. She and her brothers had been playing with fireworks. Some diesel fuel had spilled. Sunita caught on fire. She was burned on her upper chest, neck, upper arms; her chin was stuck to her chest. Her pain was unbelievable. She survived. The Sisters took her first to the hospital and then with them to the Shishu Bhavan.

Her father and brothers did not want her. She was scarred and had no value. She was now with Mother Teresa and the Sisters. She now had many mommies.

When I first saw Sunita, she had already had one surgery. I asked Sister Marcellina if I could please take care of her. I had worked with plastic surgeons at home, and I knew I could be of help.

I grew to love Sunita. I wanted to bring her home, but it wasn't meant to be. Instead, I was meant to be a part of her life—always close to me in my heart and prayers, and seeing her each time I go to India. It is a gift I have to this day. And every time I see Sunita, she's better and better, prettier and prettier.

When I go to Calcutta, she's one of the first children I go to see and hug. I feel like one of her many mommies. When she hugs me, she stays with her head on my chest. She says, "Auntie, I have missed you so much." She calls me her "God-mother."

One year, Sunita said to me that she doesn't know why a man would want someone with so many scars. Sunita, your beauty is so much on the inside that it radiates and makes you even more beautiful on the outside.

Sunita is my child, and when the right suitor comes, Sister Marjorie will know and so will Sunita.

And I will go to the wedding.

GOD'S MERCY

The Sisters at the Shishu Bhavan and I have seen the children recover so quickly—with food, love, and care. This comes on the heels of no food, sometimes no love, and little care.

What amazes me is that the recovery is total with many of the children. Lingering mental effects are minimal and rare.

Sister Marcellina said to me, "It's God's mercy, Katie. With so much suffering, mercy abounds."

Thank you, God, for your loving mercy.

AMALIA AND FARUK

She still had the glow. She was fresh from heaven. She was hours old.

I was in a hurry. I was to deliver a message to Sister Sarah Grace at the Shishu Bhavan. My mind was absorbed in the message and the verbal delivery. It was a busy day and needs were great. I needed to deliver my message and get on to the next project.

But it stopped me—that glow. In my peripheral vision, it was unmistakable. I turned. She laid there on the floor beside her young mother. She was beautiful—the glow was a halo, like a ring around the moon. A beautiful baby girl. The cord still throbbing. New life. A still peaceful silence accompanied the glow. I was a witness to a brief glance of heaven.

I forgot everything and just looked. The chaos and noise stopped, drowned out by the beauty of this glowing child.

I heard a soft whimper over to the other side and saw tears falling down the face of a little boy. He was sitting with his tiny stick legs out in front of him. He was sucking his thumb. He was very thin and weak, barely able to sit up. His tiny abdomen was round and large—bloated from lack of food; his hair was the color of straw. He was in the final stages of starvation. He was naked except for a dirty plaid shirt with all but one button missing.

How can this be? A young, hungry mother with no one. A new baby girl and a little boy so hungry he was literally sucking the skin off his red and swollen thumb.

Here is the greatest weakness for me—hungry, sick, starving children. Just seeing this is a torment that will stay in my heart for the rest of my days. Unbearable. But it exists.

Mother said … that "one drop in the ocean" …

I picked up the little boy. He sure did not want me; he wanted his mother.

The Sisters had gathered the mother and new baby and were cleaning them up. The Sisters brought some warm milk in a bottle and some bread. My boy was so tiny and sick, I wasn't sure of his age. His teeth that were in told me he was two or two and one-half. His body mass was of a one year old. God have mercy.

I have been through many trials in my life, but nothing compares to this. A hungry child … my heart shatters.

Slowly, slowly, tiny sips. He cries. He doesn't want milk. He wants mommy. Sister brings some rice. Small bits of rice. Please eat, please eat. Food for life. Please God, please God, let him live. Let him be okay.

A bath. We filled a tiny plastic tub. Sores and calluses under all the dirt. God help him. Now, he is cleaner, with a little food in that tiny swollen stomach. So little strength. Still the tears. He is so tired. He's giving in. The eyes close. He's out. So, so precious. I feel content.

The mission I was on didn't matter. This was all that mattered to me. Sweet boy. Thank God for the Sisters. You have a chance at life. Sister comes over. She holds her arms out for my precious cargo. I'm bonded and it's hard for me to let go. My beautiful dupata (scarf) covers him. Finally, the trade is made. Bye-bye sweet boy. I'll check on you later.

It was touch and go for many days. We learn his name, "Faruk." Sweet boy.

Faruk cannot hold down any food. Down it goes; up it comes. He is so very, very fragile and sick. The Sisters tell me when I visit that he may not make it. On the other side, his mommy and baby girl are doing well—"Amalia," the girl with the glow.

Each day I beg God; please let him be okay. Let him be okay. Give him a chance. I want to bundle this baby boy up. I want to take him home. If I could, I would leave India with bundles and bundles of babies.

Time to go home. It's hard to leave. So many things I will miss. Okay, but I'll return. I have to. My other life in Calcutta.

Faruk, dear, tiny boy.

I'll pray for you each day.

TRUE LOVE

[Excerpt from a November/December 1999 letter from Sister Andrea]

Since this may very well be my last letter to you in this year, let me share with you a very unusual experience ...

For the past 5-6 years, a very big neurologist has been offering his free services to our poor in the Shishu Bhavan dispensary. He must have treated hundreds of patients—children with cerebral palsy, older patients with Parkinsonism, and every kind of seizure disorders or epilepsies of various etiologies and degrees.

Last month our Sisters brought to him a young couple with a 4-year old boy. He was hyperkinetic and had a history of epilepsy, too. The parents seemed quite well off, so I asked with surprise why they came to our place which is only for the poor. Then I came to know that this was actually our child—they had adopted him from our Shishu Bhavan 3 years ago—when he was a baby and quite all right. One year later he suffered a terrible attack of fever, and ever since he developed this neurological handicap! The parents had already taken him to every big hospital in India—now they wanted to give it a last try with us.

The mother was holding the boy, but he was wriggling in her arms, utterly restless, groaning as if in pain and hitting out—the father in great distress tried to explain the facts to the doctor. For some reason the doctor asked him many questions in a rough way—perhaps he too was wondering why such a rich couple had come to him here. So we had to clarify this point, and he gave the child a full and thorough examination and then prescribed the treatment. When they were leaving, a thought came to my mind.... I went out to them and asked them privately: "Do you think this child is too great a burden for you? Would you like to bring him back to us?"

The mother's eyes widened in horror—the sorrow in the father's face deepened, and suddenly he had tears in his eyes! "Do you know," he asked with a choked voice, "that this child is the life of my life! I could NEVER be without him or give him away!" I felt so small beside them ... for even having asked such a question! And I thanked God in my heart that he had given to this father and mother the courage of a true, beautiful love. How different our world could be—if all of us accepted a little of the "burden" of each other! How it would help us to grow in love and compassion!

But thanks be to God—there ARE many people who do have that courage—silently, without big proclamation, they give their strong, deep love perhaps to an old mother who is crippled with pain, or to a little mongoloid child which during pregnancy went undetected, because they wanted to accept whatever child would come from God—or to any bed-ridden, perhaps querulous neighbor—brother—uncle—aunt, whoever! Yes, these gifts of love and service ARE THERE, they are happening today, here and now. It's just that the media are not interested.... But—wasn't it a great joy for all of us to hear that Medecins sans frontieres [Doctors Without Borders] were awarded this year the Nobel Peace Prize?

Praised be God for all this goodness!

More Silent Saints

AUNTIE ELLA AND RICKY BOY

Auntie Ella and Mother Teresa were old friends.

Years back, Auntie Ella wrote Mother and asked her if she could use the services of a just-retired woman from Australia with lots of energy. Mother wrote back and told her, "God called you to help us care for his poor in India." Auntie Ella was seventy-three years old when she first came to India.

I met Auntie Ella on my first trip to Calcutta. She was ninety-three years old.

Auntie Ella was from Australia. Each year Auntie Ella came to work at the Shishu Bhavan. She came at the same time each year—November. Everybody knew she would arrive the first of November.

There was great excitement at this time especially for one rickshaw driver. He had known Auntie Ella for the twenty plus years she had been coming to Calcutta. We all knew when it was the first of November; his rickshaw was at the Monica House Gate. The plane was heard flying over. In a few hours, she would be here. "Ricky Boy," Auntie Ella's old friend.

Auntie Ella always stayed at "Monica House." Monica House is a boarding house run by the Episcopal Church on the grounds by St. James Church on Circular Road. It is in the heart of Calcutta across and just down the street from the Shishu Bhavan.

Each morning she left Monica House, and Ricky Boy took her to the Shishu Bhavan to hold, feed, and care for the babies. If you ever wanted to know where Auntie Ella was, you looked for Ricky Boy and the rickshaw. He waited patiently for her; they were very old friends.

Auntie Ella's hair always looked perfect. She always wore a long blue skirt and a white cotton, lacy blouse and high heels. Now this may not seem unusual, but it was generally very hot and very humid in Calcutta. Auntie Ella worked as hard as any of us and she always looked great. She was always in a good mood and I never saw her angry.

Auntie Ella died when she was ninety-seven years old. She was a remarkable woman. She saved up her pension checks to buy her plane fare. One trip she stayed almost a full year. Auntie Ella always said once you have been to Calcutta, you are a different person.

Auntie Ella never liked praise.

She said that belonged to God.

KERRI'S PREPARATION

Kerri was from the United States.

Kerri was a young, vulnerable girl when she came to India. She left two months later, changed and grown far beyond her age of twenty-one.

Working in Calcutta is not what most young people seek. The work is very hard. And it's hot, dirty, and sometimes just downright miserable. And yet, each day Kerri plunged ahead doing what was contrary to her. Working day in and day out, mostly at Kalighat. And each day she grew.

Kerri loved God and wanted to serve him. She was thinking about joining the MCs but struggled with the hard life in Calcutta. Could she do it? Was she called to the sacrificial life of no husband, no children, hard work, separation from the world? And what about Patrick who she met in Calcutta and who she came to love?

All of this was answered in Calcutta.

I saw her sitting by Mother Teresa's tomb mornings and evenings. With each of these visits, she came away with more and more clarity. "Yes," she would enter the religious life, rules and all. But not with the MCs. She loved the mission and the work, but it was not her calling. She told me, "I know myself. I can't do it." There was something else for her; something that was drawing her back to the States.

Patrick, Jorge, Terin, Kerri, and me ... Kerri's last night—dinner at the Circular Hotel was so fun—such wonderful friends; each of us has changed so much. Calcutta does that. Kerri has blossomed into a giving, open, focused young woman. And it was time for her to leave.

She went back home. She prayed and discerned. She found her calling.

Kerri became a teaching nun back in her own country.

Calcutta was her preparation. And it was very good.

Janine—The Elegant Woman from St. Tropez

I was always told that most French people did not like Americans. It also seems I heard the French are rude. Well, obviously the people who say and think these thoughts never met Janine.

Janine is a widow from St. Tropez. She was eighty years old when I met her on my first trip.

Janine is cultured, lovely, well-educated, and fun-loving. Before she came to Calcutta, she had been all over the world. She and her husband had together translated books and translated for people. Janine's stories of her husband and their travels are amazing. They faced many dangers together. As a team, they spent time tutoring the royal families in Laos and Cambodia. When the Communists came in, they had to run for their lives.

Janine met Sister Fabian in Southeast Asia. Sister Fabian was instrumental in Janine coming to Calcutta. Sister Fabian is a very gifted musician, but one of her greater gifts is seeing gifts in others and encouraging them to share.

Janine was particularly distressed by the exploitation of young children in India. Many of these children work eighteen-hour days. Some work on hand-tooled leathers, or perform sewing, or other labor. Many are almost the main support of families. All of this combined made Janine more of a passionate women than she already was. It affected her enough that she got many of her wealthy and political friends involved.

Janine worked tirelessly to help the children. She spent time with the street kids in Calcutta. She would buy their leather goods and take them back to France to sell. She did a lot more.

Seven languages, all spoken fluently, this was one of Janine's many talents. Her English was flawless. Sometimes she would say, "My God, you Americans butcher the English language." Janine hated slang.

Janine and I rode the bus together on many days to work at Kalighat. Janine would say, "Today let us bathe the ladies. Then let us do some shopping; I want to buy some things for the old ladies by the hotel." So shopping we went with our Swedish and Norwegian and German lady friends. Janine spoke fluently to them in their native tongues.

At the market place, Hindi and Bengali is spoken. And guess who was speaking back to them bargaining in Hindi and Bengali?

Yes, Janine … the lovely lady from St. Tropez.

KiKe and Anna

KiKe and Anna are from Spain.

KiKe loved Anna. He met her in Calcutta. He loved Anna the minute he first saw her.

KiKe is one of the kindest, gentlest souls I've ever met. He never tries to hide or downplay his feelings. He's there and every emotion always comes forth—such a beautiful, rare quality ... so open and willing to be vulnerable.

He was generous with everyone he met. If a smile was needed, you got a smile. If you were begging or looked hungry, you got either rupees or a meal. You never left KiKe without being better off.

KiKe and Anna both worked at Prem Dam and sometimes at Kalighat.

One day, we were having lunch and he put his hand over his heart and said, "I love Anna." He said it so beautifully and strongly; I could feel his love for Anna in those three words. The most beautiful part was Anna was sitting two seats down from us. She just smiled. I was so touched by his openness and her smile. It was a treasured moment.

Anna got very sick in Calcutta. KiKe was very worried. She got better slowly, but KiKe got very sick. He almost did not get better.

I think that he asked God to give him what Anna had so she could get better.

Could anyone have a better friend?

AMIT'S SILENCE

Amit came to Calcutta before returning to his home in Tel Aviv, Israel.

He was twenty-one years old and had just served his time in the Israeli Army. There, when a child is six, they begin training in the desert.

When you first meet Amit, you are startled by how handsome he is. He is even more beautiful on the inside. Inside and outside, Amit was beautiful.

I had the privilege of working with Amit at Kalighat.

He did not talk a lot about what he had experienced in the army, but the unspoken words spoke volumes. He was working through a lot at Kalighat.

He told me that when he was younger, he had met Mother Teresa very briefly. This short meeting affected him very much. He knew he wanted to come and work with the poorest of the poor in Calcutta.

And so he did. For Amit, it was a dream come true.

I believe that Amit's soul went home to Israel in order, thanks to Mother.

NOEL'S BIG HEART

After our first meeting in the early hours of the morning on the streets of Calcutta, Noel stayed on and worked at the Shishu Bhavan. She loved the children and they loved her. Noel would arrive in the morning and sit in the middle of the floor. The children would flock around her—Noel is incredibly beautiful, inside and out.

Noel held babies. She fed babies. She thrived. Her heart was so big. It was hard for her to leave Calcutta, but it was time.

More of India was calling. To the north and west, Rajasthan. A stop, a family, a home for a time.

It was in Rajasthan that Noel met Anar and her three young sons. They lived in a hut and cultivated a cilantro field. It was very hard work. And the pay? About twenty dollars a month at the most.

Noel adopted Anar and her family.

With her big heart, Noel wanted her adopted family to have a real roof over their heads. She went to the Indian Bank and got five hundred in U.S. dollars worth of rupees. In rupees, that is a huge stack of bills not easily hidden. It was also dangerous for Anar. Her mother-in-law could abuse her and take it or she could be threatened by the men.

Noel left India and went back the States. She returned again to Calcutta, to see and work with Mother Teresa.

She then went north and west to Rajasthan.

Anar now had four sons. And they had a cement house with a floor and a roof.

Thanks to Noel and her giving heart.

TEA BREAKS

I was making a cup of tea tonight. I don't like tea; I only like tea when I'm in India. This tea tonight was being made as a skin tonic. Tea has a lot of value for me as a toner for my skin. White tea to almost a boil, steeped, and used all week.

In the US, it's my toner. In India, it's my tonic. Indian tea cannot be duplicated in California. I know that it is imported around the world, but it is not the same as when you're in India.

Indian tea breaks are heavenly. The cup of tea is like a meal. The taste is, well, it can't be copied. Water boiled, tea steeped—cream, sugar, lemon. Oh, it is wonderful!

In India, tea is a strength ... a morning break at the Shishu Bhavan or Kalighat. More than tea—it's a social time, a cool break from held back tears, visiting with friends, expressing our days, discussing events, debriefing, emotions shared. Sharing the emotions and tears that result from what we have seen, done, or experienced ... sharing with our friends, the Sisters, and God.

Life simply lived and shared all in twenty minutes—new friends, new lives, fears expressed, deeper bonds.

Tea breaks, prayer breaks, new beginnings.

MOTHER'S ROBE

One year when I was in Calcutta, Mother Teresa was very ill with heart problems. Her Sisters surrounded her. It was thought Mother would not last the night.

Sister Marcellina was at Mother's bedside and asked Mother if she could have a piece of her habit. We Catholics love anything attached to a saint. Mother Teresa said, *"Yes."* So the Sisters cut up her habit, the clean one, leaving Mother with only one habit.

The next day, Mother was in the chapel bright and early. She never stops.

I was working that morning with Sister Marcellina. We had to drive one of Mother Teresa's ambulances on an important mission. While riding in the back with Sister, she took out a large piece of cloth. I asked her what it was. She told me that it was part of Mother's robe. WOW! And then, even better she said, "Would you like a piece?" Oh my, yes!!

Thank you for this treasure ... a true relic ... a piece of cloth touched and worn by a living saint!

Another special day in Calcutta.

The Indispensables

LUCKNOW

Tonight my friends from Spain, Anna and Maxura, are taking many of the patients from Kalighat to Lucknow, a city in Northern India.

In Lucknow, the MCs have a home for those unable to care for themselves. If you are handicapped, mentally ill, or bruised and broken; if you are young or old, without a home, or simply have need of a little love or a place to stay … you can come for a day or as long as you like.

This was a most welcome place for the Kalighat patients who recovered—no sitting around, but grounds to walk in and Sisters to spend time with them. And, there was food to fatten the reed-thin ones, such as our dear Narian, the fifteen-year-old boy who nearly died of the brain malaria. We thought he would never survive … and then he was joyfully taken to Lucknow. When he got fatter and healthier, he went home to his mother and brothers.

Thank you, Mother Teresa, for saying "yes" to God.

To your many calls within the call.

THE GHANDI SCHOOL

Before Mother Teresa started the Missionaries of Charity, she taught the young girls of Calcutta. Several of her former students joined her as her first MCs.

Sister Franchesca was one of them.

Sister Franchesca is in charge of the Ghandi School. She helped to found the school back in the 1970's. It is located in the center of Calcutta just a few miles from the Mother House. The school serves many needs and solves many issues. Like Titagarh, the name speaks volumes; Mahatma Ghandi, the Indian "great man of peace."

The Ghandi School teaches children who cannot afford to go to school, or young adults, perhaps uneducated, so they can make a living. Many young volunteers come and teach language, reading, and writing skills. And if you need a meal, a small shed always has food available.

The school is also a haven. There was once a family with a young girl. They were living on the streets in Calcutta. The police came and broke up their temporary abode. The Sisters found the three-year-old girl alone, crying and with no clothes, separated from her family. They brought her to the Ghandi School until … the happy ending; when parents and child were re-united.

One year, I visited the school with Sister Andrea. It was November 30th, a day full of blessings and surprises. It was Sister Andrea's feast day! I was fortunate to be included with Sister Franchesca when she honored Sister Andrea at the Ghandi School—all the children sang for her feast day; it was so special. Auntie Ella was there, too, and she gave the children candy and balloons. So, so simple; but how much those children loved the treat. I wanted to cry, but tears didn't belong.

Another sanctuary in the heart of Calcutta ... where love abounds.

And all are welcome.

IT ALL HAPPENS AT THE DISPENSARY

Food, medicine, clothes, blankets, whatever you need ... you can get it all at the Dispensary.

Located next to the Shishu Bhavan, it is a beehive of activity from the early hours of the morning and throughout the day—yet another site in Calcutta from which the Sisters serve the poor and their needs in so many different ways.

And "the team" is in charge! Sister Andrea and Sister Shanta. They take their work very seriously and yet are always full of *joy*. They are two of my closest friends in Calcutta.

As the head of all that goes on at the Dispensary, Sister Andrea has little time. And yet you would never know it. An MC and an MD, problems are solved, situations are delegated, impossibilities become possible. Sister Shanta is the master of all that comes in and goes out. Everyone who comes there has a card; everything is hand-written. No need for a computer, Sister Shanta has a computer disk in her head; she remembers everything and everyone. Mention a name, an incident, a history ... no buttons to press; she knows.

When I think of the Dispensary, I think of a lot of things, but especially the medicine and critical medical supplies that are stored there. Maybe that's because I'm a nurse. Or maybe it's because every time I come to Calcutta, Sister Andrea asks me to organize and re-organize all of the supplies.

I also think of the trips to the villages especially the ones every Tuesday and Saturday—"mobile clinics" for hundreds of the poor in the outlying areas of Calcutta. Supplies are prepared and organized throughout the week for these trips. And, there are certain days that are set up at the Dispensary where the poor can come there and see the MC Sisters who are doctors; Sister Shanti, Sister Andrea, and Sister Michael. Or the specialists that volunteer their services, like the neurologist in Calcutta, an old friend of Mother Teresa, who still comes every Friday.

At the Dispensary, the Sisters also mix and prepare medicine and distribute it to the poor. And bandages are boiled, re-used, and re-wrapped. But it is more than a "dispensary."

Blankets and other supplies are received and given to all those who are in need. And food is provided to the poor every day. Lots of food. Early in the morning, the Sisters begin cooking rice and dal in those *huge* pots. They serve two to three hundred, or more, of the poor and hungry every morning with the lines starting to form long before the sun rises.

Whatever you need, Sister Andrea, Sister Shanta, and all of the Sisters at the Dispensary will do their best to help.

NOVICES TO NURSES

Oh yes, and another thing about the Dispensary ...

The MC novices learn here. They become nurses overnight or in a day or two. I have been privileged to help in their training. Every year I come to Calcutta, Sister Andrea sends me a whole new set of Sisters to teach ... sometimes as few as two or as many as ten in a group.

The first day, it's "basics" ... hand washing, germs, bacteria, blood pressure, lung sounds. Simple things to do when necessary. Day two is graduation day—injections, IV, IM's, medicines.

It's a gift to me; such a wonderful treat to teach eager young and older Sisters. They are so happy and fun-loving, giggling ... and scared, too. All this joy wrapped up in them, and this is the way they will serve the world.

I may teach them simple things, but they have taught me so much more.

Make your work a joyful prayer. Joy to the world.

That's the MCs.

THE VILLAGE

Every Saturday at the Dispensary is set aside for "the village."

This particular village, unlike the Tuesday village located just outside the city limits, is about an hour and a half drive from the heart of Calcutta. People come from miles around; from all over the region. Every Saturday. Everyone knows the Sisters will be there.

Many people walk for days just to get medicine or food or fill some other need. None of these needs is small. It's an enormous task. No one is turned away.

Preparation is always ongoing at the Dispensary for the trips to the village. But on each Friday night and Saturday morning, the preparation is finalized. A huge truck, an old WWII army tank, is loaded with food, medicine, bandages, blankets, and supplies. Then after the truck is packed, we all hop up in the back of the truck and find a place to sit on top of the supplies or on benches that are set up in the back.

"We" means volunteers with medical backgrounds and the Sisters—Sister Andrea, Sister Shanta, Sister Shanti, and the novices.

I helped in the preparation for these trips, and I went to the village almost every Saturday I was in Calcutta. I looked forward to it.

When we arrived, we were always greeted by throngs of Indians—anywhere from three hundred to eight hundred of the poor and needy. I remember the first clinic of my first year in Calcutta—I was proud to see that much of the rice we gave out said, "United States of America."

In the village, you saw everything: polio, TB, cancer, burns, malnutrition, worms, scabies, lice. When you looked out at the sea of faces, you think of the impossible. But impossible is not an option in the village.

One year before Christmas, there was a particularly enormous crowd. I said, "Sister Shanta, we cannot do all this." Sister Shanta said, "We will do it, and it will be done well."

Well, as usual, if God wants something done, it is done.

We not only took care of everyone and everything, we were finished sooner than expected.

PRAY FOR ME

November 30, Feast of St. Andrew.

Tonight before adoration, such a profound gift ...

Sister Nirmala was leaving for one month to go to Africa. For the last two days, I have been wanting her blessing but didn't want to bother her. She is so quiet, a true contemplative. Last year, my daughter and I had the profound gift of meeting and spending time with her. She is so kind and humble. As I was coming around the corner to the Mother House, the Sisters were escorting her to the car. I stepped aside but one of the Sisters said, "Get her blessing," and Sister Nirmala came to me and touched me, gave me her blessing, and then said, "Pray for me."

I will pray for you, Sister Nirmala. Adoration was full of peace for me; it was offered for Sister Nirmala ... and for Sister Andrea on her feast day.

God bless them both and all the Sisters.

And thank you, Lord, for a glorious day.

Give Until It Hurts You

SIMPLICITY = FREEDOM

So many things have crowded into my mind and heart but today, since arriving, I am finally able to begin the journey ... the writing down of this, my fifth trip to India.

As I have known for well over a year, God has wanted me to return here to Calcutta. So, after much planning and much letting go, I have rid myself of more of my worldly possessions, including the Mustang convertible. It's a very freeing thing to shed oneself of material things. My only treasures are the people of the world I dearly love.

It's simple; if you haven't used it or worn it in a year, give it away or find someone who needs or wants it. My house is no longer full of "stuff." It used to be.

After my first trip to Calcutta, I followed Mother Teresa's advice. I wanted to share, to give. I came home and downsized and simplified.

And I did it again.

And again.

It feels right and good. You don't have all that "stuff"—extra baggage to worry about. I think over the last ten years. I've furnished lots of homes with things that I didn't need or want or wear. The outcome? Well, for one thing ... less dusting, less laundry, and less work.

The best simplification came during one year when I had no money, but I had time ... and I so badly wanted to go to India.

I had a garage sale to end all garage sales. It all went ... and so did I—to India.

Lightness. Simplicity. Freedom ...

... to give more of oneself, to love more completely ... to be open to God's call.

THE FORTUNE COOKIE

I had Chinese food one day.

I opened my fortune cookie. It said, "As the purse is emptied, the heart is filled." According to this cookie, my heart is overflowing.

Ever since my first trip to India, Mother Teresa's words continually have played over and over again in my mind and heart, "*Give until it hurts you.*"

Every time I come back to the States, I eventually finding myself wanting to go back to India. I want to be that little drop in the ocean. And so, as time has passed, my home has become my trip back to India.

The bank asked on my loan application why I was taking cash out again. "It's only money." "You can't take it with you." "I'm spending my children's inheritance." "I'm homesick for India." "I don't mind if it hurts ... it has to hurt." These are things that you can't put on the application.

My friend, Father Ed, once said to me, "Katie, the Brink's truck will not follow you to the grave." How true.

Give until it hurts you.

And the more we give, the more we receive ...

... of the things that really matter.

THE FIGHTING IRISH

I can't explain it; it sometimes starts out slow—a quick longing—then flashes of India. Sounds, smells, scenes, an ache, then a full blown "gotta go."

Besides … trips to Calcutta always give me back the pieces of my heart that get chipped away living a hectic life in America.

Mother Teresa asked me once, "Where is your home"? Before I answered the question, I wondered for a moment: where *is* my home? The answer is: wherever people you love are—that's home. Or home is where the heart is. So my answer was, "California, USA." But the real truth was California and Calcutta where I leave a giant chunk of my heart.

The "gotta go" really hit me in 1995, but I had little money. The hustle and bustle was absorbing me, and all I could think of was Calcutta. Even a quick trip, a month, would really hurt financially, but didn't Mother say, "Give until it hurts you"?

This trip would really hurt. I knew it would bring me closer to that one day that I knew would come. But for now … it was time for a garage sale and a few shifts, and a phone call to Linda, my "travel agent." Given my limitations, Linda got me the *cheapest* ticket you can find; the ticket was a real bargain. I left a week later on a newly-formed Russian airline. San Francisco, London, Tajikistan—if it was safe to land, and if we do, keep your blinds down—then New Delhi. A change to Indian Airlines, and then home to Calcutta.

I had called the Missionaries of Charity house in San Francisco and said, "I'm going to Calcutta; can I bring anything?" Yes, some special books, letters, important medicines, and a few boxes to be given directly to Mother Teresa. Packed heavily, I left.

London check-in was a little out of the ordinary—a make-shift booth for the new airline in Heathrow that didn't look as if it fit. The thought came to me, "You get what you pay for." I got a bit nervous looking at the man behind the booth; "sinister" was the word that described him.

"Well Miss, so you are traveling to India. I see you have many things to go directly to Mother Teresa and letters. Perhaps they contain money. If you wish to take these articles, pay us an extra five hundred US dollars." The smile never left his face. I told him that I do not have five hundred dollars, but these things are priceless and can mean nothing to you. Besides, this is for the MCs. "Well, unless you give five hundred dollars, these articles will stay." Extortion! Blackmail! What could I do? Please, I beg you, if I had the money, I would give it.

I left the line. What to do? I went upstairs to the chapel at Heathrow and begged God to intervene. I went back in line again. I could see the Calcutta treasures with the five hundred dollar price tag. Sorry, I'll go, but I do not have the money. The smile left his face. My boxes for Mother were left by his feet. I felt betrayed. God, are you going to allow this? Where are you? Gate call for Tajikistan and New Delhi. The lounge in the waiting area felt like a box. I was crying; this was so terrible. What would I tell Mother and the Sisters?

An Irish accent interrupted my thought. "Miss McCloskey, we at Aer Lingas heard your dilemma. Hide these tags; these are your checked bags for Mother Teresa. They were taken and put directly into the aircraft. When your blackmailer was finishing the flight, we moved in. Say a prayer for us in Calcutta."

My people—the Irish!

It was a proud day and a lesson. "If God is for us, who can be against us?" He did hear my prayer in the Heathrow Airport.

I told the story to Mother Teresa and the Sisters when I delivered the boxes. One of the sisters said, "Katie, I fear for that man with his evil plans." Sister's fears were justified.

I got stranded in New Delhi on the way home.

The airline went out of business in the time span of two weeks.

Another adventure … with God's purpose and plan being fulfilled.

NEW DELHI ... THE LONG WAY HOME

Before I left Calcutta, I prayed, "Lord please, the trip here was traumatic. Let it be smooth on the way home with no drama. No incidents
please; let it be smooth sailing."

Wrong prayer. Well, Calcutta to New Delhi was fine, the usual airport hassle and drama, but tolerable. Even the taxi to the international
terminal went smoothly. However, that's when it started. I couldn't
find my airline or gate. It turns out that when I was in Calcutta, my
airline went out of business—wiped out, gone, not even a trace. I felt
my mouth go dry. And it came to me once again, "You get what you
pay for."

Well, here I was. The lady at the information booth could not even
remember the airline's name. She told me that I would have to buy
another ticket; my return ticket was worthless and there wasn't an airline anymore to get a refund. I felt alone. I turned around and looked
into the eyes of another bargain airline shopper. Sam and his wife, Barbara, who was in a wheelchair, had the same tickets. We were the only
people who didn't know. Great! Sam and Barbara were returning to
London. I looked at Barbara in the wheelchair and could see that she
was really not well. Nurses have a trained eye and we can see a lot in a
glance.

We became instant friends and were in this together. Barbara was
lying in the chair. Sam told me they had traveled all over India for two
months. They sold their home to make this trip. Barbara had cancer
and all that could be done for her was done. Before she died, Barbara
had a heart's desire, a wish to see India. They had little money but Sam
loved Barbara. The house was sold, and they went to India. Sam said
that up until about a week ago, Barbara did well and was very happy.

Then the pain started, and she just wanted to return home. Now this. Barbara was getting weaker by the hour.

I always travel with "extra" medicines. The nurse in me always likes to be prepared when one is far from the conveniences of Western medicine. I thanked God for my mini storehouse. It was meant for Barbara, and God knew what lay ahead for her.

The information booth lady said, "Well, I will call the airport manager. This is bad timing for you. There is a holiday coming and everything is booked. You can't stay here as all the hotels are booked."

The airport manager was very accommodating; for fifty dollars each, we could discuss flights out. "Everything is booked. but we will try." But you know. Inside, I was becoming angrier and angrier. God help me! And God, please give Barbara the strength to return home. The angrier I became, the calmer Sam became. He bargained; he paid. But still, "Sorry, everything is booked. Your wife, sir, if she is ill, we cannot let you leave."

Then I became calm, and Sam blew his top. We got out of New Delhi fourteen hours later on our way to Bombay and then to London. Barbara slept most of the way home. She was comfortable; she was holding a miraculous medal that Mother Teresa had given to me. I told her of my India and Calcutta. We landed and they were home safe. I just made my flight to San Francisco—smooth sailing all the way back.

Barbara died the day after returning home. Sam called to tell me the news.

He told me that Mother's medal never left her hand and she was buried with it.

I had to work extra jobs to pay Sam back as he bought the tickets.

But it was well worth it—the time I had with Sam and Barbara could not be replaced.

You get what you pay for.

And sometimes you get much, much more.

TRUE WEALTH

I knew the day would come ... the price tag attached to "give until it hurts you."

Each trip to Calcutta was costly, and mortgages have to be paid. Banks don't believe in charity, but the call to share was greater than the security of money. Don't get me wrong ... I love money, as it gives me the "freedom" to do as I wish. I love pretty things. I love good food and wine and nice places. If I had never shared, I'd probably be not too bad off. And maybe have extra money to do "whatever."

Now I own nothing. The house is gone; mortgages and frequent trips do not mix too well. My house was old and costly. It was becoming a worry and a burden.

We look at people today and say, "Wow, he has it made. Money, nice house, nice car, everything, the true American dream." But what is wealth? There is a scripture verse that says, "For what will it profit a man, if he gains the whole world and loses his soul?" (Mt. 16:26) Not a good trade.

Mother Teresa and the sisters have changed the way I view life. My first trip was an initiation. My Western lifestyle seemed excessive and selfish. My thoughts turned into a conversation with Mother Teresa and started the simplification, the sharing, the giving.

Now I term wealth in the story of one little boy. Faruk.

Eight months have passed and I am back in Calcutta. I went to the Shishu Bhavan. I searched the rooms. I talked to the mashis and the Sisters.

"Katie, maybe he didn't make it."

"Oh, Katie, come here." Yes, I recognize him. He is sucking his thumb.

The impossible happened, something I never would have thought in this time span. He had acquired the body, mind, and looks of a healthy three-year-old child.

I only recognized him because he was sucking his thumb. The piece torn from my heart when I first saw him is now replaced. I went to him, knelt down and picked him up. He snuggled into me and rested his head on my shoulder, sucking that thumb the whole time. Who is this strange woman? He doesn't know me, but I know him. Inside my heart is a spot, and his name is written there. Faruk.

From the brink of death to a new beginning.

Now that is true wealth.

A New Way to See

There is a term that I do not like. It's called "letting go."

What does this really mean? It's often used so lightly … something like, "Oh, just give it up," or "It's a piece of cake," or "So what."

For me, if I have to "let go" of something, it's often not a "piece of cake." It's usually a long, drawn out, and very painful process.

When I go to Calcutta, my "letting go" becomes a list.

But it's different here.

I see things every day that cause immeasurable suffering. And I am easily able to "let go" of my burdens, the things that are troubling me. I see the things that are really important.

One day before evening prayer, I had a quick sit-down talk with Mother Teresa. She looked at me intently, took her hand, brought it up, and made the sign of the cross over my left eye. She then said, "Come. Let us go and pray." No other words. No explanation.

Two Sisters came by and asked me, "Why did Mother bless your eye?"

I had no answer.

But I do know one thing. Since being with Mother and the Sisters in Calcutta, I see everything differently.

Everything.

And More Silent Saints

PEDRO'S TRADE

"Katie, only one beer ... it will help your immune system and clear out the Calcutta dirt from your throat."

That was Pedro's advice. I have followed it each trip I've made to Calcutta. One beer—the recipe for good health. Like an apple a day. It works every time.

Pedro is from Majorca, a beautiful island off the coast of Spain. I vividly remember the day I first met Pedro. You can't easily forget meeting someone like him.

It was dusk and something had brought Sister Andrea out of the Shishu Bhavan and the Dispensary. We were walking a short distance and talking about Saturday and going to the village. The streets were more crowded than usual because the Feast of Kali, a Hindu holiday, was beginning. I didn't see Pedro approach us as I was shouting to Sister Andrea above the din of the street noise. I remember turning to look at a small band going down the street with all of the festivities behind it.

The next thing I knew, Sister Andrea had taken my hand and put it into a man's hand and shouted, "Katie, I want you to meet my dear friend, Pedro." All of a sudden, I was looking into the eyes of one of the most handsome men I have ever met, and I heard no noise. I had no tongue. I was stumped. Time literally stood still. After a few seconds, he began talking to me. I don't remember what he said, but we agreed to meet with some mutual friends the next evening.

Pedro has been a dear friend ever since. And yes, he is beautiful outside. But what is even *more* dazzling is what is *inside*.

Each year in November, Pedro comes to Calcutta for two months. He leaves behind beauty and a wealthy lifestyle. He comes to filth and poverty. He trades Majorca for Calcutta. Total opposites.

Prem Dam, the MC's home for the elderly unwanted and unloved, is Pedro's favorite. Pedro walks each morning through the streets of Calcutta to arrive at Prem Dam. The day begins at seven-thirty a.m. Bathing, feeding, washing, sweeping. Hard work physically and hard work for the soul.

Before Calcutta, Pedro had a different life—all "fun" and not much work. He met Mother Teresa. His whole life changed; to sharing and caring.

Pedro is a very private person. He shares little about life before Calcutta. And yet, it is clear that the world is much different now for Pedro.

From riches to poverty.

Each November to January. Pedro's favorite months of the year.

PATRICK ACCEPTS

What a huge blessing to be with Patrick and others like him. Their goodness surrounded me, and I have taken little bits of them with me that will last the rest of my life.

Patrick is from Switzerland. He is one of the sweetest and kindest persons I know. Rare and good qualities in a man. It was easy to see how Kerri could fall in love with him.

He is also a chef and a champion ice skater. Patrick loves to cook. When he joined the Swiss Army, they made him a cook. I imagine the troops were grateful. Patrick has a unique gift—you just want to be around him. He's always smiling; always. And the smile envelops you.

Patrick worked at Kalighat and Prem Dam. He taught at the Ghandi School. He helped everywhere. And one year, Patrick got sick, oh so sick—bad headache, backache, nausea, fever. Malaria only shows up in a test when you have a fever. I took his blood up to the City Lab for Sister Andrea. Patrick's high fever produced the dreaded result—malaria. The ever-ready smile was still there but mostly only in his eyes. I helped to nurse Patrick for a week while he regained his strength.

Patrick then told me, "Katie, I'm going to go home to Switzerland and tell my family that God is calling me. It will be hard for them, but I know I am to be a priest."

A higher call.

Dear Patrick, what a gift you are to the world … and to God.

And to Austria. Patrick now serves there as a priest.

HILDA AND THE PRIESTS

Hilda was from Baton Rouge, Louisiana. She married John late in life and was widowed shortly after they were married. Like Esther, she had an excess of love. Hilda wanted to put it into action.

I met Hilda on my first trip. It was hers, too. Hilda was eighty years old.

Hilda spent much of her time working at Kalighat, bathing and caring for the women, doing dishes, cleaning. This was not easy work for a *young* woman. Hilda showed us what working hard really meant.

Hilda knew everyone in Calcutta, especially the priests. One afternoon, I accompanied Hilda to the rectory of St. Theresa's, the parish church just up the street from the Shishu Bhavan, to deliver a message to Father Joe. It was a lovely visit, and I was very happy to be included. Father invited us both to return the next evening for dinner … a great honor for two women. I was thinking, "How nice to spend more time with Father Joe and Hilda."

We arrived for dinner. Father Joe was at the head of the table. Hilda was seated at the other end. I was seated in the middle—with six priests across from me and three priests on either side of me. It seems that a number of guests from India were visiting … thirteen priests total, twelve of them surrounding me.

The priests at St. Theresa's had a cook. He was Indian. He was not excited about the surprise guests. He had to make dinner for all of us—thirteen priests and two women. The look on his face spoke volumes. As soon as the meal was on the table, he was out the door like a bullet.

It was a very quiet dinner, although there were a lot of smiles. I didn't know what to say. The Hindu language barrier was a bit of a problem for both Hilda and me—neither of us spoke it well. I felt that maybe with so many priests, I should start confessing all of my sins, past and present.

I spent a lot of time looking at my plate. I remember everything to this day: rice, three boiled potatoes with two boiled onions, Indian bread, and a glass of water.

I'm sure Father Joe and the twelve priests are still telling stories about the dinner that night ... with the two quiet American women.

JORGE'S LOVELY BLACK CURLS

Jorge is from Chile.

He is a very gifted young man, especially in language skills.

I liked spending time with Jorge. He was fun and funny and spoke almost fluently in Hindi and Bengali after just standing and listening. He was humble, too. If someone laughed at his pronunciations, he laughed, too. Then he asked the person mocking him if he would please help him.

Jorge taught at the Ghandi School, and also worked wherever the MCs had a need. But what I remember most about Jorge is his lovely dark head of soft black curls.

One Saturday when we were working in the village, I noticed Jorge's hand constantly in those lovely curls. Scratching again and again.

The dreaded head lice.

After we were done caring for the villagers, I called Jorge over for an examination. The malady always looks as though sea salt was poured on the head; these are the eggs. Then you see the monster daddy; he is a medium brown, with eyes on little stems and the jointed legs with stick-um feet. Oh my, oh my, and yes, they do jump.

We treated Jorge on the spot.

The next day I went to the market. I bought Jorge a comb, shampoo, and more medicine—and some treats, because he wasn't happy about this situation. As I was walking back through the market, I ran into Patrick. He said he would come along with me for Jorge's last treatment. As I was unpacking the market goods, Patrick said, "For heaven's sake, Katie, it's not his birthday. He has lice." Well, so much for Jorge's treats. Patrick ate half of them.

Patrick and I arrived. We examined. We had to tell him. "Jorge, it's bad. We have to shave your head." Jorge said that his mother wouldn't like it. But he knew it had to be done. Those lovely black curls.

Jorge grew immeasurably in Calcutta. So gifted, and yet so humble.

I knew that he and Phinula—she was from Ireland—really liked each other. I thought they might get married one day.

But Jorge also had a higher call.

Jorge is now studying in Rome for the priesthood.

THE FORMATION OF MATTIUS

I first met Mattius in Calcutta back in 1995 when he was a young medical student. At the time, he looked like he was about twelve years old.

Now, Mattius is in his thirties and a pediatrician. He has also matured into a very handsome young man, although sometimes I tell him that he still looks like some of his patients.

And he has a heart of gold.

Mattius is from Germany. He is Sister Andrea's nephew. He comes each and every year to Calcutta to work with "his Auntie" and all of the MCs in Calcutta. Mattius spends his days mostly at the Dispensary and the villages. He is gifted and needed.

Mattius was formed by Calcutta. It was his learning ground, his formation for becoming a doctor. Mattius brings his skills to Calcutta. And then he takes Calcutta back to Germany. He says he has a permanent soft side because of the conditions of the children, what they endure in India. It is unprecedented and so difficult to comprehend in Europe and the States.

When I see Mattius with the children and babies, I am so glad he wants to share.

Sister Andrea is so proud.

Her nephew is part of the fragrance.

THE LOOK

Certain moments stand out. They are poignant. You do not forget them.

I was waiting outside the Mother House on Lower Circular Road. My back was turned. I was watching for my friends Pedro and Mattius to come down the road.

I heard commotion behind me. I turned around, and Mother Teresa was coming out to get into a minivan to go on a mission somewhere. Our eyes met for a brief moment. No words were spoken.

I felt in her look as though she knew … not only where I was going, but who I would become. She was seeing what Calcutta was doing to me.

She smiled at me.

Mother's smiles … they made you feel as if you had just shared a brief, wonderful secret.

A Very Special Ministry

A DIFFERENT WAY OF LIFE

Sealdha Station, Howrah Station ... these words bring disturbing images and memories. Train stations in Calcutta are not like train stations anywhere else I've been. Wall-to-wall people, a sea of humanity, huge trains—iron monsters—zipping in and out, noise, filth, garbage.

And used as "dumping grounds" in Calcutta for the unloved and unwanted.

Young children like Meena and Narian, women like Prem Bhora's mother, and so many others of the poor in India.

It is a very special ministry to "work" at Sealdha and Howrah. "Working" at these train stations means going there in the morning and becoming the hands, eyes, and ears for God and the MCs—seeking out the sick, the lonely, the dying, the abused, the babies, the abandoned—and then caring for them ... bringing them to Kalighat, the Shishu Bhavan, or one of the other MC's safe havens praying for the right outcome.

It is hard work.

It requires much courage.

It cannot come from oneself, but only from above.

PREM BHORA

Prem Bhora in Bengali means "full of love."

I held Prem Bhora in my arms. I had to come to see this young baby. She is upstairs at the Shishu Bhavan in the most fragile ward. She is cared for, fed frequently, and held often. I met her mother. She's at Kalighat, a patient, a young wounded soul—very broken, inside and out.

Prem Bhora's mother was found at Howrah Station. She was beaten severely. She had been taken to the train station. Her husband brought her there. She needed to earn money; he sold her to a man. She refused. Her husband and the man became angry. They beat her and threw her down. Abandoned to die, but found. Inside her clothing was a tiny, thin baby; very weak, almost a newborn. Prem Bhora.

I was often sent by the Sisters on "special missions," bringing messages from one of their havens to another. One day, I was going to bring some supplies to Kalighat. Sister Joan of Arc at the Shishu Bhavan told me the story about Prem Bhora and her mother. Then she asked me to relay a message to her mother: "A decision is needed—do you wish to keep the baby?"

God give me strength—I could never give up one of my children.

I went to Kalighat. As I sat with Prem Bhora's mother, I looked into her eyes. I relayed the message. I was holding her hand; she was holding mine tight. Corrie from Holland and two Sisters were with me and they were holding and comforting her also. She began to speak of things that shattered me to the depths of my soul ...

"When I was five, my father took me to the train station. I was sold to men. When I was older, my father married me to a man who also sold me. I know nothing of anything but this. I do not want this for my daughter. I give her. Her life is to be different from mine. I gave her life; I give her up. Please take her."

Prem Bhora's mother smiled. She has lived an unbelievable life of abuse. Yet she remains in a way "untouched." There is a softness and an innocence left. I am in awe of her courage. She is giving up her child for a better life.

Sister Paeline, the assistant head mistress at Kalighat, promised that her child will never be returned to her former life; the Sisters will protect and care for her.

I went back to the Shishu Bhavan and spoke to Sister Joan of Arc who was holding Prem Bhora. I cried. But then we both smiled. Prem Bhora was smiling. We stroked her tiny face.

Sister said, "Let's pray for them." We prayed for them.

I will always pray for them. They are permanently embedded in my heart.

CARMEL: FABULOUS AND FEARLESS

Carmel is from Ireland.

When I first met Carmel, she was nineteen years old. Carmel is young, fabulous, and absolutely fearless.

Carmel has an old head on her shoulders—a rare quality in a young woman. She also has street smarts, a soft heart, and is truly wise beyond her years. Carmel is a wonder.

Carmel works at Sealdha and Howrah. While few volunteers work at Sealdha, even fewer work at Howrah. Even though she was not Indian, Carmel knew the people she needed to know at the stations, and they all liked Carmel. She could speak the language; she could communicate. It was critical to the work.

I met Carmel at Kalighat. I had a patient in bed #7 who had many wounds. The patient right next to her, in bed #8, would swear at me in Hindi the whole time I was doing wound care or work on the patient in bed number seven.

Carmel arrived at Kalighat early that morning with two new patients. We were having a conversation, and I began talking about the patient in bed #8 cursing me each time I began my care for the patient in bed #7. Carmel relayed to me the following story:

"The State Hospital is right next to Sealdha Station. Although they are both 'dumping grounds,' the difference between Sealdha and the Hospital is—with the Hospital, you may never get out. Many of the Hospital patients are mentally ill, and were brought and left there. Some of the long-term clients are women whose husbands or families wished to be rid of them. Anita, my bed #8 patient, was in this category. Anita's place in the hospital was on the second floor. She had a corner by one of the bathrooms; it was literally an open grate to lean against. Many times, because of the location, people went to the bathroom on her. Once a normal woman, in this environment, Anita lost her mind."

Some of the volunteers and others knew of Anita. They went in and wrapped her up and brought her to the Sisters.

The last time I saw Anita at Kalighat, she was smiling.

THE STATE HOSPITAL

I have been inside the State Hospital.

It defies description. It's almost more than the spirit can comprehend.

I was only there for about fifteen minutes. It was like a slow motion picture. Small children on cots. Old dirty dressings on infected wounds. Deep puddles of urine to step over. Moans. Crying. A heavy feeling made worse by the knowledge that lives are lived entirely in this place.

I recall seeing one woman with a broken hip, a leg never set had its home there. I saw her dirty cot. Her bathroom was the floor underneath. She grabbed my hand as I went by. No words, but the look spoke volumes. I learned afterwards that somebody came in and carried her off. No one missed her at the Hospital.

Fifteen minutes ... more than one lifetime lived.

CARMEL RESTS

Carmel works unbelievably hard. But my most vivid memory of her will always be in the chapel in the Mother House. Adoration time starts around six or six-thirty p.m., depending on the day. During this heavenly hour, the rosary is prayed and then there is prayer time in front of the monstrance—Jesus in the Blessed Sacrament. Come and tell him everything.

One night, Carmel came in, sat in a corner, and closed her eyes. In minutes she was sleeping with the most peaceful look on her face.

During the day, she works harder in Calcutta than almost anyone I know. Now, God was surrounding Carmel, and she was resting in his presence and loving arms.

She earned it.

KIM—ANOTHER LIFE CHANGED

Kim and Clare were friends from back home in Georgia.

Young and energetic teachers, they came to Calcutta together—both Southern Baptists, both women of God and wanting to help the MCs with serving the poor.

Like Clare, Kim was special.

You know, "special" is a word that signifies so much. I don't know if special is a good enough definition of Kim. One of the first things you notice is her beautiful eyes; dark brown, but how the light shines through. She radiates God's love. Her heart is so big, and it feels and absorbs so much. Kim's heart was completely opened in Calcutta.

Kim worked at Sealdha Station. One day, she found a young woman there, about twenty-five years old. She probably weighed fifty pounds, if even that. Kim and some other volunteers brought her to Kalighat in a cab. The young woman was so weak, she could not even hold her head up. She was so happy to be with us. We started an IV on her, but we were really too late. Her life ended two hours later.

Kim cried and cried. She told me she felt responsible. She felt that if the woman had been found the day before, she might have lived. It took a long time and many tears for Kim to recover.

What effect did this young woman have on Kim?

Kim continued to work at Sealdha. She became stronger. She brought many persons to Kalighat including our young Narian.

Kim went home to Georgia with Clare and back to school. Today Kim is a physician's assistant, and she shares her talents and skills with others. One year, Tajikistan was fortunate to have her.

She who has received, now gives.

I just got a letter from Kim. She longs for Calcutta.

HOWRAH AT CHRISTMAS

December 23, 2003
Hello all,

Thank you so much for your Christmas wishes. Well, Christmas here is certainly a million miles away from home. It would be perfectly easy to ignore Christmas if one so wished (of course, I'm not letting anyone forget, constantly singing Christmas songs). It's completely non-commercial and my Indian friends tell me that Kolkata is the only place in India where Christmas is really celebrated. It being India, Christmas is celebrated more for its spiritual side. There are a few shops with Christmas decorations though. There's no Santa Claus here. But again there is definitely some Christmas spirit in the air. Again everyone is walking around wishing each other Merry Xmas, etc., and we've been doing loads of extra work in the spirit of the season.

Last week we went to Howrah Station at night to deliver blankets. It was a wet and cold rainy night. I had to fight back tears at several points. I see these people every day, but at night they are even more pitiful. It doesn't matter how much they laugh during the day or how proud they are, at night they still sleep in the dirt covered up in rags. There were two occasions where what we thought was a heap of rubbish turned out to be an old lady. It was awful seeing young developmentally-challenged boys huddled up under bridges. They are so innocent and so unloved. The families, the children, the old women and men, the beautiful old man I helped on a train to god knows where; they are all so clear in my mind and have definitely made a deep and lasting impression on me. It's hard to describe because I feel that to verbalize it diminishes the experience.

Two days ago we distributed 150 food packages to the kids in Howrah Station. I thought the girls would tear me apart grabbing for food! The boys were beautiful though. On Indian trains they have little boys who *sweep the floors, then ask for money. Some of these little boys saw me giving food to the station kids and asked me for some. When I told them to come with me to platform eight and that it was chicken, their little eyes lighted up and they ceased to be these soulless pitiful creatures ... and [they] became the beautiful smiley little boys that they are so seldom allowed to be. They couldn't have been more than five or six and they grabbed my hands and made a song about chicken. Again I was deeply moved and deeply ashamed.*

After we gave out the food packages, Martin, Bert and I went and bought the kids from Shishu Bhavan Howrah (the orphanage I originally worked in) toys and chocolate and music and Colgate and soap. Then we picked up 300 blankets from Kalighat and brought them to my flat. I wrapped up the toys and brought them to the orphanage the next day. I spent a wonderful morning with the kids. Gosh, I really love them there!

Well, it's Christmas Eve now. We have the play this evening. I'm so nervous. After the play, we have Midnight Mass, a bite to eat, then my co-workers and I stay up all night distributing blankets. Then we return to the station and work as normal. My only dilemma is whether to go to Prem Dam or Kalighat for Christmas lunch. I'm not sure what I'll do for the actual day. I guess I'll go for dinner somewhere. I'll probably just sleep the day away!

Anyway, may God bless you all this Christmas and may you be filled with all the love that life has to offer you. Merry Christmas!

Love, Carmel

"Back Home" Silent Saints

MY NEIGHBOR JACK

I want to remember to e-mail Jack, my neighbor.

Jack has colitis and is in constant pain. He always asks me before I leave for India how he can help. He often has medications he does not use, and he gives them to me, so that I can give them to those in need.

I have to tell him how I used some of his Percocet, a pain killer, for the man at Kalighat who had the whole top of his leg gone. Jack, in his generosity, unknowingly spared him pain before I did his dressing change. The man's response from the pain was lessened quite a bit … thanks to Jack.

Just one of the many gifts Jack has given to India.

From back home.

DR. JOHN: "IT DOESN'T GET ANY BETTER THAN THAT!"

Five hundred dollars.

Perhaps not a lot here in the United States, but *so much* in India. There, it buys an open heart surgery. Well, maybe not now, but ten years ago it did. As my friend, Dr. John, a general surgeon, used to say, "Hey, it doesn't get any better than that!"

I worked with Dr. John at a small hospital many years ago. He actually made house calls. He had beers with his patients. He also could have a bad temper when things went wrong.

And Dr. John had a big heart.

When his early morning surgery patients came by on the gurney, he would tell them with a huge smile on his face, "I just had a great big breakfast ... bacon, eggs, pancakes, lots of butter, and, oh yes, fresh-squeezed orange juice." His patients laughed, if they were able, or at least smiled, even if they couldn't eat. They loved him.

If his patients couldn't pay, Dr. John many times let the bill go. Erased, clean slate, nothing owed.

Dr. John started a free clinic for migrant workers at a local school fifteen years ago—it's still alive and doing very well.

Since my very first trip to India, whenever he knew I was leaving, Dr. John would say, "I want to give you some money; here's a hundred dollars. Say 'hello' to Mother Teresa for me." Then, before I would fly to India, I would always get a nice letter from Dr. John telling me not to drink the water ... along with another pile of money. The first year, he gave me five hundred dollars.

Dr. John's patients may not have had breakfast when they were in his hands.

But lots of people in India ate because of him.

ANNE AND THE SOAPS

When I wash my hands with any sweet-smelling soap, I think of Anne. To know Anne is to love her. Anne and I are hospice nurses and have worked together on and off for many years.

I've told Anne many stories of India, but she was especially concerned about the fact of soap being expensive in India. And this fact alone had its effect—cleanliness. Many of the street children and adults needed soap. It's precious in Calcutta. A simple thing for us but not for the poor. Many will sell the other half of the bar of soap for a few extra rupees. Anne couldn't deal with that.

When I pack for India, every space is utilized mostly with medicines or small necessary things. I buy all my clothes when I arrive in India. This one year I had soap. And not just plain soap, beautiful soaps—thirty bars of all kinds of soaps.

When I arrived, I unpacked. Each day I took five bars with me, and each day five people got a bar compliments of Anne.

One little boy and his mother were by the side of the road begging—both thin, both in need of a bath. A bar of the beautiful rose soap came out. I said, "This is from Anne, little boy." His mother was so happy, it was as if I handed her a diamond.

The next day, I saw them both clean and I saw a half-bar of soap with their meager belongings. Next to the half-bar was dried milk and some biscuits—the price of the other half-bar of soap.

Food for the little boy and his mother.

NICOLE, JEANETTE AND MARGARET

"Katie, can we come over? We want to see you before you leave!"

My dear nurse friends. Nicole, Jeanette, Margaret. Believe me, if you ever get sick, you want these three women at your side. They will help you to heal, solve your problems, and be there for you as you get better.

There is a lot of love wrapped up in these ladies. They have families, bills, issues, but before each trip, they take the time to come over to send me off with love and prayers ... and money to feed the babies of India.

When I'm in India, the same movie plays. This time, it's a good one. I sit and am feeding a child or adult, thanks to Nicole, Jeanette, and Margaret. I can't wait to return to tell "the girls" when I get home about who they helped. And they love to hear the stories.

My hands. Their hearts. God's work.

NOEL MEETS MOTHER

Noel had been to India two times. On each visit, she had missed seeing Mother Teresa by hours.

In 1996, I was leaving for Calcutta. I called the Sisters in San Francisco to ask if I could deliver anything to India. "Oh Katie, no thank you, but Mother Teresa is here on a private visit and will be going home soon. You will see her in Calcutta."

I knew I had to call Noel. Maybe she hadn't yet seen Mother Teresa in India, but perhaps she can see her in San Francisco.

Noel arrived in San Francisco an hour after I phoned her. She rang the doorbell at the convent on Fulton Street. "I'm sorry dear, but Mother is having a private visit with the Sisters." The door began to close; Noel saw Mother Teresa walk by as the door was closing. She was crushed.

But then the door opened, and Noel was invited into the chapel with Mother Teresa and the Sisters as they prayed.

Mother Teresa made room for her, reached out, and took her hand, "Come close dear, let us pray."

Another prayer answered.

MOTHER'S ROBE AND CHINA

Kathleen is a friend of mine. Maria is Leo and Kathleen's adopted daughter. Maria is from China.

One of Mother Teresa's heart's desires was to go to China to open a convent. Each morning in the chapel of the Mother House in Calcutta, a special prayer was said to the Mother of God, "Virgin of Shen Shen," for this miracle to occur: a Missionary of Charity home in China.

It almost came to pass before Mother's death, the visit to China. Mother Teresa was flying to San Francisco to see her Sisters. A high Chinese official was on board the flight. They were seated next to each other, and there was a glimmer of hope. It could be possible. This man would try to intervene. Maybe Mother could come and see.

The Chinese government rejected the project.

Kathleen and Leo had waited for a year for permission to travel to China to pick up their new daughter. The time had come, and the orphanage where they were to get Maria was right where Mother Teresa had wanted to go.

Mother Teresa had died, but I had a piece of her robe. A piece was cut. A part of Mother was going to be in China. Kathleen clutched this piece all the way there. In the excitement of the adoption, she almost forgot. In the last moment, she remembered.

And a piece of Mother is buried on a hill by an orphanage in China.

Mother Goes Home

LETTER FROM CALCUTTA: SEPT. 19, 1997

My dear Katie and Linda,

I hope you are all well. I thought of you many times and never wrote. Well, I did once to give to a friend of Katie's, but I somehow missed her. I'm sorry.

Thank you so much for the beautiful writing paper and for your photos and letters. I can still remember receiving that parcel. Sister Bethany gave it to me in adoration after a day that hadn't gone very well—your kindness brought me a lot of joy, especially to know that you were praying for me. We all need each other's prayers so much. I think I've put all the photographs in a book—they are wonderful—all the different aspects of Calcutta, different homes.

I'm sure your hearts have been very much with us these last weeks, with Mother going to Jesus. It has been a sad loss but at the same time, we are being constantly reminded of Mother's presence with us more than ever and of the necessity of continuing the work she began according to her calling. Mother herself wrote these words some weeks before:

"Time has come closer. Mother also has to go to God. Then Mother will be able to help each one of you more, guide you more and obtain more graces for you."

Her last words were, "Jesus, I love you. Jesus, I trust you. Jesus."

On the tomb in Mother House is written simply, "Love one another as I have loved you."

Our priest, Father Larry, yesterday told how after a conversation with Mother, she suddenly turned to him and said, "I can't believe that God would be so humble as to love me." *Please pray for the Sisters especially—everyone is feeling the loss of Mother. I know you do, too.*

I must return—about 5ᵗʰ November. I'm still praying but I think I may come back after a month, here, to Kalighat, God willing. Please pray for me—I need prayers.

With much love,

Tania

THE DREAM

Before Mother Teresa died, I dreamt of her. I was in California. She came to me with her smile and her hands slightly outstretched and she said, "Thank you." The dream stayed vivid.

When she died two days later, I was sad that I had lost a friend. But I had heard her say goodbye, and I knew where she was going.

To heaven ... her true home.

A REAL LAMENT

My daughter and I were in San Francisco when news of Mother's death came. Linda lived there at the time and worked with the MCs on Fulton Street.

We bought some flowers at a tiny market—lovely blue hydrangeas and some sweet-smelling tuber roses. We went to Fulton Street for the holy hour at six p.m.

We rang the bell and took our place on the carpet. Mother's picture had been placed there, and all the candles were lit. Our hearts were like rocks. The air was heavy with sadness. Mother was gone. We knew where she went, but it's hard for those left behind. The world is a lesser place now. A great saint has gone home.

The doorbell rang again and again. It was mostly news reporters. The Sisters said, "Please come back tomorrow; tonight we are praying."

Lament can be a very deep word. It considers all the person was, and the emptiness that is now there in the person's place. Even still, Linda and I felt our hearts lighter when we left Fulton Street that night.

Mother Teresa had taken a part of them and had lessened our sorrow.

ONE YEAR LATER

This morning's Mass at the Shishu Bhavan was extra special.

Today was the Archbishop of Calcutta's fiftieth anniversary, and he was here. It was also the feast day of St. Therese, Mother Teresa's patron saint, and so, Mother's "feast day" as well.

The Mass was always special at the Shishu Bhavan, a reminder of when my daughter, Linda, was with me in Calcutta. It's also a reminder of home and how much I miss seeing everyone. I believe it would be good to go home at Christmas for two weeks.

After the Mass, the children danced downstairs for the Archbishop. It was so dear, and one thing stands out … the song … "One little, two little Indians…." At home, it would be impolite or too ethnic, but here it was very touching.

One year since Mother passed away. She is missed.

MOTHER'S TOMB

Mother Teresa is buried in the Mother House on Lower Circular Road. It's in the heart of Calcutta. Her tomb is a raised marble bed with a simple inscription of Jesus' new commandment from St. John's Gospel, "Love one another as I have loved you."

I remember October 1, 1998. All the Sisters came later in the day to the Mother House to be by Mother's tomb. To spend time with her on her Feast Day.

I felt so peaceful there beside her and the Sisters, but also I felt a great heartache. Perhaps I felt how much she was loved and just how much she is missed.

Each morning and evening I was in Calcutta on this trip, I would go and pay my respects. But I ended up sitting down and talking just like I would if she were sitting and listening to me.

It's very calm, quiet in the room.

And I know Mother is listening. How? Well, I've had too many prayers answered after my visits. I feel like it's a direct phone line to God.

I say, "Hello God, hello Mother Teresa? You know I need your HELP!"

And then help is on the way.

MOTHER'S BEATIFICATION ... VIVA LA PAPA!

October 19, 2003. Rome.

Viva la Papa! Viva la Papa! Long live the Pope!

I heard the crescendo rise and fall. Again and again. I had chills from the top of my head to the tips of my toes. Like Mother Teresa, the Holy Father had a quite a presence. I felt it before his motorcade passed me.

A wave. A smile. There he is ... another special vessel of God's love; spreading His fragrance.

Pope John Paul II was going through the crowd after Mother Teresa's beatification ceremony. Here was "God's representative," and you knew it. You felt it deep down in your heart, your soul.

The process of Mother's beatification was "sped up" by this Pope. We know why ... miracles giving glory to God after her death. Beatification is a key step on the path to being declared a canonized saint, and the Church is wise to declare it carefully.

Mother's ceremony was spectacular. I wouldn't have missed it for the world. The MCs gave me an invitation. Plane ticket purchased immediately. It was said that there were three hundred thousand people in St. Peter's Square. I believe there were many, many more. The ceremony included traditional Indian dance and customs with Indian music.

Mother Teresa would not have liked the attention, but she would have loved the ceremony.

Mother Teresa did amazing things with God's help. She was his arms, hands, legs, and feet. But especially his heart. She affected all our hearts.

Mother Teresa, in the eyes of those who knew her, had long before arrived at sainthood. The title was earned and given before she left this earth.

We all saw and knew that she truly was a living saint.

PHOTOGRAPHS OF MOTHER

I have always marveled at Mother Teresa's patience.

She was gracious even when mobbed by well-meaning visitors.

She hated her picture being taken. I heard a story from Sister Colette that Mother Teresa asked God for a soul to be released from purgatory each time her photograph was snapped, knowingly or unknowingly.

So with that deal made, I believe many souls met Mother Teresa on her arrival in heaven and said, "Thank you, here's your photograph."

I also took a few photos of Mother Teresa. I always asked her permission. She always nodded *"yes."*

One time she was standing outside her office. She turned and waved to some of us standing below. All the cameras came out. I had mine that day. I raised my camera and she was looking right at me, but I couldn't do it. No permission. My arms went down.

To this day, I have a vivid picture of Mother in my heart and mind.

And I don't need a photograph to see her.

A Picture of Love

Puja Holidays 1999

My dearest Katie,

How have you been? Are you coming soon to India? *** All of us send you our loving greetings.

◆　　◆　　◆

I am sure that you are aware that our Mother House and the whole commission are working hard on gathering all the "witness material" for our Mother's cause. I had heard many times about some canonization processes here and there, but I never knew how interesting the whole thing was, and what a tremendous amount of work has to be done for it! Of course, people tell us—WE KNOW that she is a saint, so what is all this fuss about? But for us—this is like a discovery journey into the richness of Mother's spiritual life. Thank God, Sr. Nirmala said we are not in a hurry at all—let us reverently and gratefully enter into this spiritual legacy, our Mother's deep life of union with Jesus. I feel very privileged to be called to be one of the "Witnesses"—but I also pray much, because we must take an oath to speak the truth, the whole truth and only the truth—as we see it. So help us God. In the end what I see emerging is a beautiful mosaic of the Face of Jesus himself—a picture of love which our Mother painstakingly wrought, collecting carefully and placing one little stone next to another—acts of trust and faith and love in a harmony of colours. And we are all part of that great picture! Isn't that wonderful?

◆　　◆　　◆

We are looking forward to a Special New Year—and we must start it with special new hope and courage. Who knows where the Spirit of God will lead us—there are tremendous possibilities! I'm sure when I hear from you again, there will be plenty of Good News, and we shall praise God together for His love.

Let us then celebrate a beautiful Advent, preparing for a truly Christ-filled Birthday of Jesus, and a powerful start into Anno Domini 2000!

With much love, and remembering you daily in Jesus,
Sr. Andrea, MC

P.S. Have you heard that Calcutta will soon be known as "KOLKATA"? Smile ...!

Reflections

HIS EYE IS ON THE SPARROW

India has become for me the place where my soul and spirit rest in God and find direction and peace—within myself and with others. All this while serving him in the way I love most—sharing my nursing skills. As each day is a new beginning, so each day in India is a lifetime of growing and learning; seeing God's mercy in action.

Yesterday, I was riding with the Sisters in Calcutta in Mother's ambulance searching for morphine for someone in great pain. I saw the likes of which I have never seen before … unspeakable living—filth, dirt, the foot-and-a-half dead rat lying on its back. It's hard to put into words. And so many people living in these conditions. What are their chances?

Walking to the Shishu Bhavan I said, "God, what will you do with India?" As it ever is in India, it seems he answers right away.

I looked over and saw three tiny sparrows searching for some grain by the wet, slimy gutters. It came to me: "His eye is on the sparrow." Reflect on this.

I did, and it came to me.

"And not one of them will fall to the ground without your Father's will. But even the hairs of your head are all numbered. Fear not, therefore; you are of more value than many sparrows." (Mt. 10:29-31.)

I had my answer.

THE CHANGE

I wish I could describe the growth of the soul in Calcutta. It's like the miracle of a seed sprouting in barren soil. Here, life is not normal. Yet you are growing even as you are trying not to see, smell, feel or hear.

And since the eyes are the window of the soul, you are changed. It can't be helped.

You can go once and go home early. You can come back over and over again. Either way, you are never the same.

And what's the name of this growth?

God's call—followed.

THE BEAUTIFUL GREEN SHAWL

Regret. This word does not convey one thing enough—an opportunity missed.

I had just purchased a beautiful shawl for a friend back home. It was olive green with embroidery around the edges. Warm and well made, I found it at Entally marketplace. The price was also great—around three dollars, a little over a hundred rupees.

As I left the marketplace, I crossed over to see the Sisters at the Shishu Bhavan. Lying on the sidewalk was a young woman having a rest.

This would probably be her home for the evening or a day or a week. The sun was going down and it was getting cooler. She was thin. She had no covers and only a light, dirty dress on.

I had the beautiful shawl.

I wanted to cover her up. But then I thought, "No, somebody will steal the shawl." I had a whole text going on in my mind. Instead of just doing what was "best," covering her up, I didn't.

I regretted it; I still do to this day.

And the shawl?

The friend I gave it to did not like it that much.

THE MOON

When my daughter Linda and I returned from Calcutta in 1997, we told God over and over just how grateful we were to be home. The clean air and water, and being with family and friends added to our thanksgiving.

The first night home, we were very tired and went to bed early—at opposite ends of the house. At the stroke of midnight, we were both awakened at the same time; the moon's brightness was blinding with its rays streaming in through the windows causing us both to jump out of our beds.

It was as if the moon was dancing in the sky. Beautiful fingers of light reached in and touched us.

We met and stood upstairs together enjoying the moonlight and continuing to thank God for being home ... and for waking us up to enjoy his beautiful creation.

LET GOD LOVE YOU TOTALLY

Father Tom is from England. He is here in Calcutta on a mission and for a conference. His sermon this morning at the Mother House was simple and direct. It penetrated many hearts.

Including this one.

How many times have we heard, "God loves you." We know it, we believe it, but for many of us, we still think that it may be conditional. We try to be good, follow the rules, behave, be charitable, don't speak badly of anyone, fast, pray, do things the right way. We try. We fail. We have our shortcomings, we miss the mark. We sin.

How can God love us?

Father Tom's message? Simple. "Let God love you totally." There it is. "Totally" Everything. Sins, faults, failings included. Totally. We are who we are. The full package. God loves us *totally*.

Today, I will let God love me totally. And I will love myself totally.

As Father Tom said, "It is then that we are free to love others."

INDIA AND GIFTS SHARED

In India, one's gifts and talents come to the surface. Personalities mellow. People change. Hearts are mended.

You cannot touch the starving, broken bodies of the poor without your own soul being healed—without your life being changed.

Sharing your gifts ... you receive much more than you ever give.

KNOWING MOTHER

I often saw Mother Teresa each day when I was in Calcutta. I knew her, and she knew me. She gave me a legacy. She showed me the way by her actions. So many of us are and will never be the same.

Life turned around like a river changing course. "Behold, I make all things new." (Rev. 21:5)

I continue the journey, Harry on his, Jeremiah, Carmel, Janine, Amit, all of us weaving our tapestry of life.

Mother and the Sisters and the poor gave us a lot of thread.

Spreading the Fragrance

TALENTS & GIFTS

I read once that our talents and gifts are known to God and are instilled in us before we are born. They are to be used in the world for the betterment of all. We are not to waste them by not using them. We are, instead, to share who we are and what we can do and what we have been given ... and to do it all with humility.

As Mother Teresa would say, "I'm just a pencil in God's hands."

Lord, thank you for Mother's words and for the talents and gifts you have given me—the ones I know and the ones I am beginning to learn about.

Dear God, forgive me for wasting time in not sharing your gifts before.

And help me make up for this in these later years.

Abundantly bless the people who lost out because I didn't give.

THE POWER OF A PRAYER

I used to have a fear of speaking in public. A huge fear.

It seems that most fears develop when we are children, manifest themselves in young teen years, and become full-blown phobias when we are adults.

I had dozens of excuses to get out of any speaking. I was a veteran. Ask me to speak, and I could draw from the vast storehouse and get out of any situation that threatened my phobia bubble.

But that one Sunday Mass in Calcutta was the beginning of something new. God wouldn't let me use any of my excuses. He wanted me to work through my fear, to learn, to grow ... and Mother Teresa knew it.

Mother's one prayer for me healed me and led me on to another ministry ... a new calling.

When I returned home from Calcutta after Christmas the year that Mother asked me to read at Mass, I was asked to speak at Grace Episcopal Church in St. Helena, California. My dear friend, Father Mac, called and said, "Please come and share with us about Calcutta."

I said, "Yes."

I spoke for twenty-five minutes. It was the beginning of many talks ... at schools, churches, civic groups ... to men, women, teens and children ... I was being asked if I could come and share.

Throughout the years, I have given many talks, and the more that come to hear, the easier it is for me.

If I had remained trapped in my fears, I wouldn't have been able to share. And the stories and experiences in Calcutta God allowed me to have would not have opened other hearts and minds to share what they have to offer.

A prayer—try it, it works.

God always hears.

PICTURES THAT SPEAK A THOUSAND WORDS

My teacher friends over the years have invited me to come and speak and show my slides of Calcutta, of India, to let the younger generation know how the majority of the world lives. I've spoken to all ages of children on up to young adults, including many religious education groups and classes of all faiths. I've also spoken to older groups, women and men, the Rotary Club, other civic groups and organizations.

Each of my receptions is different. But the endings are always the same.

Life-changing.

I never plan a speech. The slides are enough. Each photograph I've taken says more than I can.

One year I was invited to a social studies ninth grade class. I walked in with my slide projector and slides, and I got "the look" … you know, "Prove to me you are not the fool you appear to be."

When I began, even the class clowns became quiet. Each young girl and boy in this class was genuinely concerned that poverty to this extent exists and that young people their age were dying.

The letters I receive after these talks speak volumes. It's not me that does it … it's God and Mother Teresa and the Sisters and the people of Calcutta.

Maybe some of these souls will end up going to Calcutta, too.

October 17, 2001

Dear Katie,

I just wanted to thank you soooo much for coming in and talking to our class! This summer I was on vacation in Germany and ended up in the hospital for two months sick with a "staff infection," pneumonia and endocarditis which is a heart infection that came from the staff because like the little girl in the video I have a hole in my heart. Anyways, I'm on vacation, I ended up in the clinic and sharing a room with a little girl about nine years old. Her name was Amira and she had a brain tumor. She was flown in from Saudi Arabia and couldn't speak a word of German. I ended up helping this little girl and I really grew to love her. I'd help her eat, try and play with her and painted her nails. She died about three weeks after I arrived and I felt like I had lost a part of me, I barely knew her but I loved that little girl like she was my baby and she was in a way I was the only person she had. Her family was at home and she was all alone. This really inspired me to help more children, I did your presentation I think later on I really would like to get involved. Thank again!

Dear Katie,   3-23-02

    I really thank you for the address of the Missionaries of Charity in Calcutta, India. It was very nice and especially nice because you sent it the next day. This came as a surprise to me but I am deeply thankful. Perhaps it is just, how the Missionaries would have done it punctually yet cordially while still helping hundreds of people. This is the way that I would one day like to be. So once again I thank you for my first lesson in the ways of Charity.

    My parents and I talked very seriously about me going to Calcutta, and after close consideration my parents decided that it would not be a good idea. My mother is British but she was born not far from Calcutta in some other city, her father was stationed there in the Royal Engineer Corps. She said that she could not bear to send me back to India because she has no fond memories from there. She was disgusted with the way that people were treated there. She said that I could go as soon as I turned 18 but that it was not possible for this summer or any other in the future until I was 18.

    However, I was wondering since I speak Spanish almost fluently. I was hoping I could go to a Spanish speaking country where there were other Missionaries of Charity. I also spent 3 months in Mexico learning the language and the culture and working on a Rancho outside La Paz Baja Sur, Mexico.

    I was wondering if you could do me another great favor and send me the address of the Missionaries of Charity in South or Central America or Mexico. Or even another institution of Charity in one of those places that you know about. I wish to put my skill with working and my Spanish together as one. So please send an address.

        Sincerely,

1)

10/17/01

Dear Katey McClaskey,

Thank you very much for showing me the slides of all the pictures that were taken when you were on your trips to India. Just something as simple as showing me a slide show lets me realize just how lucky I am and how much I should be grateful for. After seeing that, I realized that I shouldn't whine as much and that I should be happy. I have never actually have been to India and have seen the pain those people go through. After I saw those slides, I felt really bad, not just for the people, but I felt guilty because I realized how much I complain about everything (stupid things that don't matter). Well, one, I'm a teenager, and two, I'm a girl, and teenage girls complain. I just wanted to thank you for coming to our class, and I appreciate how you opened up my eyes.

Sincerely,

10/10/07

Dear Ms. Katey -

Thank you so much for coming in and talking about working with Mother Teresa, and how you helped all those people who needed help.

You changed my mind around so much about how things are in India, this is true as soon as I got home I looked around my room and saw so much stuff I didn't need at all, I do come from a rich family and do have money and if I could I would some day maybe donate some money to the charity.

I have been to a lot of places in the world and now I want to go to Indea for a while.

Well I got to go, thank you for coming in.

Sincerly -

At Bandel

Amalia

Auntie Ella

The Pigs

The Joy of Work

Glow of Love

Church at Bandel

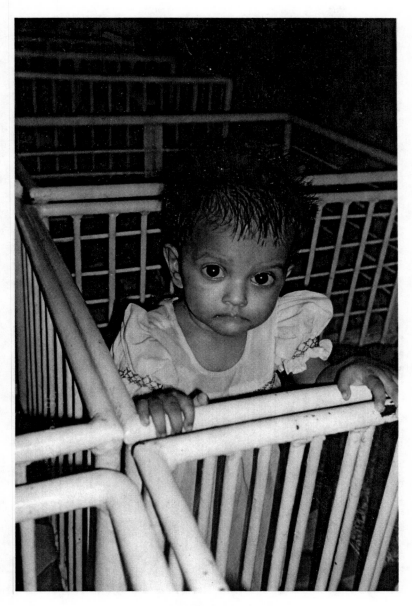

Child at Shishu Bhavan

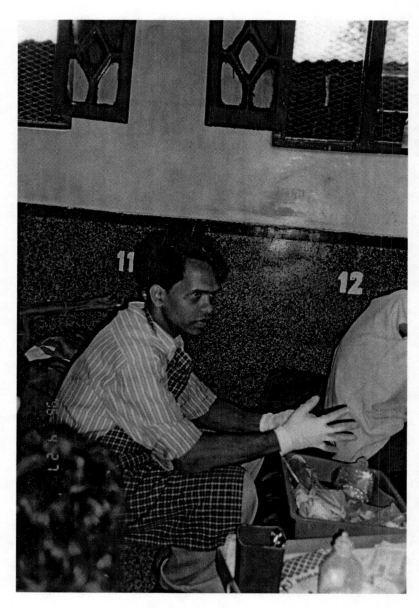

Missionaries of Charity Brother

Kim and Clare

German Consulate

Door at Mother House saying that Mother Teresa is in

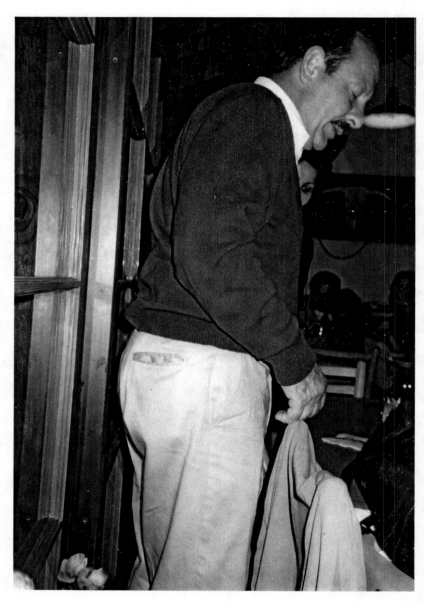

Dr. John Sweeney

Dr. Linda Sharp at Georgetown

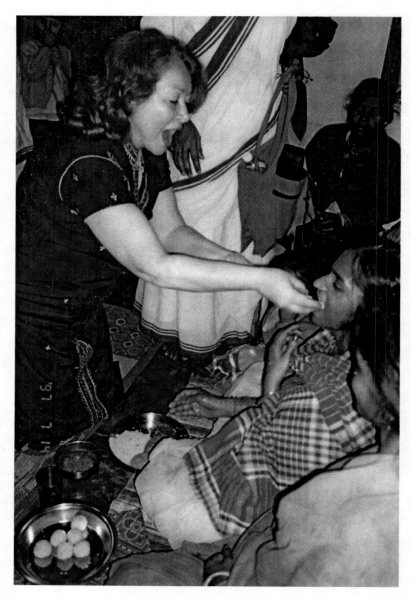

Sunita's engagement party with author

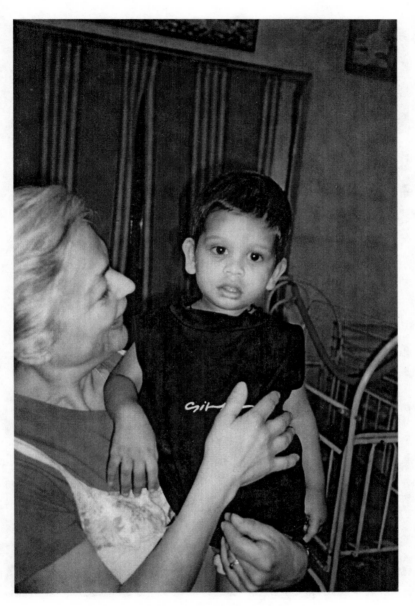

Faruk at the Shishu Bhavan

Fr. Ed Litavec

Sunita's flower girls from the Shishu Bhavan

PREFETTURA DELLA CASA PONTIFICIA

CAPPELLA PAPALE
presieduta da Sua Santità
GIOVANNI PAOLO II
per la Beatificazione di
MADRE TERESA DI CALCUTTA

Ingresso: dalle ore 7,30

domenica 19 ottobre 2003
Piazza San Pietro ore 10

01971

Invitation to Rome and The Beautification Ceremony

Kalighat

Sunita and Lawrence on their wedding day

Linda at the Shishu Bhavan

Little Boy and Grandmother

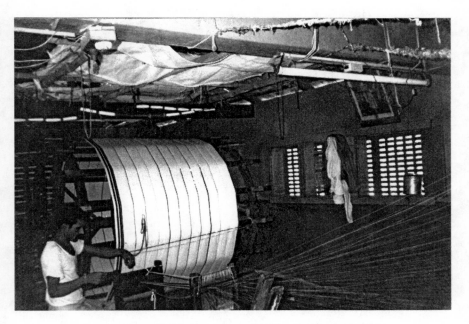

Looms at the Leper Colony where cloth for the Sisters' habits is woven

Mother Teresa's tomb in the Mother House in Calcutta

Mother Teresa after heart attack back at work blessing the volunteers prior to work

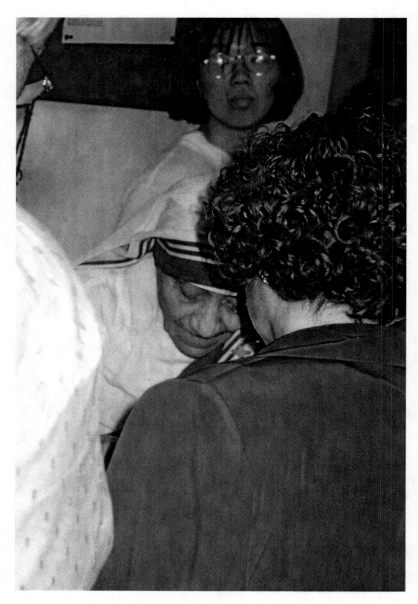

Mother Teresa passing out medals among the visitors

At Prem Dam

Receiving an award at The Leper Colony

Passing out the miraculous medals

Headstone on Mother Teresa's tomb

New novices

Paul

Bandel pilgrimage

Rome and the Beatification Ceremony

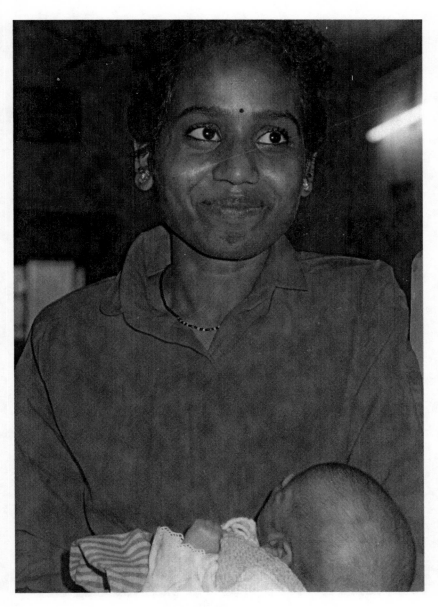

Rupa (Mashi)

Sister Nirmala

Street children

Tanya at Mother House

Sisters, babies, and volunteers at the Shishu Bhavan

The village

The Jesuit priests at Kalighat

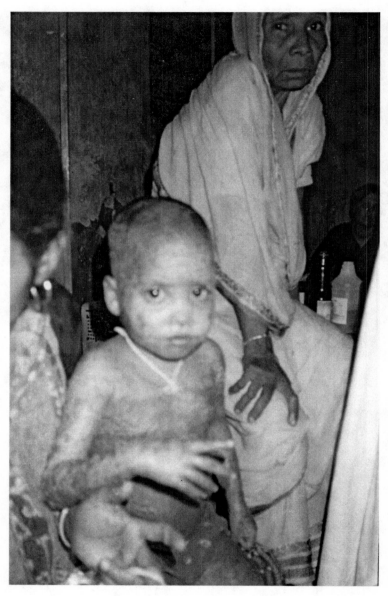

Child at the village, multiple skin problems

Going to Paul's house before the lights went out

The Tsunami

DECEMBER 26, 2004

I passed the monitor at the Amsterdam airport. Breaking news from the BBC: "Earthquake hits Indonesia." My mind immediately started racing, "This is not good."

Twelve hours passed. I arrived in India ... I was excited—I was going to Sunita's wedding, but something felt different in Calcutta. It hung in the air.

I ran to my hotel to register and then ran to see the Sisters and Sunita. I was greeted, and then the stories, the aftermath. I was stunned.

Asia has been forever changed, moved. The tip of India was gone—the beautiful Andaman and Nicobar Islands, some deep below the Indian Ocean.

I met with Sister Nirmala; she gave her blessing once again for the book. She was leaving immediately with another Sister; she described their mission to help. I wanted to go along. "I'm a nurse—please take me, too." Sister Nirmala said, "*Pray.*" I promised to pray. I prayed.

Watching the news, I prayed some more. Gathered with friends, we listened, we cried. My friends were fellow nurses and doctors, volunteers—a plan developed. In bad situations and crises, I always think of Sister Andrea's words: "What to do?" Whenever she said these words, she always had a plan. Our plan: we will go to the consulates of our countries to register and offer our help.

I went to register with the American Consulate and contacted Doctors Without Borders, and other organizations. Ten of us—all ready to go, chomping at the bit, prepared, trained. We were ready to provide aid to the city of Chennai. On the ocean, badly hit. We had a plan.

The Indian government refused. Western help was not needed. They could handle it themselves, they said.

Father Ryan said, "Katie, a good way to make God laugh is to tell him your plans."

Sister Andrea said, "Katie, there is enough suffering here in Calcutta. We need you here."

So … "my plan," maybe a good plan, maybe not. But definitely not God's plan. Letting go of Chennai was difficult, but God knows the desires and intent of our hearts.

I saw the Sisters in Calcutta planning. Their love was ready to be put in action in the city. I saw rice and biscuits, blankets, and medicines, all piled high and ready to go. God's plan was in place.

I'll come back.

And, there will be plenty to do.

THROUGH THE ROOF

The Nicobar Islands. The MCs have a convent there.

The tsunami struck.

The water was up to their necks. If it rose any higher, they would drown. The door was sealed as tight as a vacuum. There was no escape.

"Help us! Somebody help us!"

The people on the Nicobar Islands came to help the Sisters. They scrambled up on the roof. A small opening was made.

Could the Sisters come through the roof? Too much weight and everyone would perish.

Several of the smaller children became the lifeline. Slowly, slowly, small hands and feet held each other and became like a long rope. Each Sister was pulled to safety.

Through the roof.

Small hands became God's hands.

THE CHALICE

Sister Shanta shared another story about the tsunami and the devastation, the lives lost.

In a coastal village of Ceylon there was a church. Communion was being given. The church was full. People were standing in line to receive. A Missionary of Charity Sister was at the Mass. She was holding the chalice. The first wave of the tsunami hit. All were swept away.

The next day the bodies were swept back. All were naked, stripped of their clothes.

The Sister's body was also swept back.

She remained fully clothed in her habit with her hands around the chalice.

It was still in her hands.

It was miraculous.

The bishop had her buried ... still holding the chalice.

Epilogue:
God's Work Continues—What
They Are Doing Now

SISTER SHANTA'S SURPRISE

Before leaving Calcutta in January 2005, I spoke to Sister Shanta. I was sad at the prospect of not seeing her, Sister Andrea, and the rest of the Sisters for awhile, not knowing when I might come back to India again.

I said to her, "Sister, maybe you will come some day to San Francisco." Sister Shanta's response was direct and clear. "No, Katie, that is almost impossible. I will probably never leave India."

Five months later … an early Saturday morning in June. The phone rang. My "caller I.D." said "Missionaries of Charity." I answered, and a voice said, "Katie. I have a big surprise for you. Our dear Sister Shanta is here."

What??!! The other end comes alive again as the phone is passed …

"Katie. I am here in San Francisco. It *is* me. When can you come? Today?"

Well, what was "never" to be was happening. I went to San Francisco the next day and spent three hours with my dear friend and the Sisters at their house in Pacifica—a surprise donation that replaced their home on Fulton Street. A new place for them to love and care for men dying of AIDS, drugs, or alcohol. The visit was wonderful. The next day, my son and grandson came, too, meeting Sister Shanta and the Sisters for the first time. Family meeting friends, and friends meeting family. What a rare treat and joy.

Sister Shanta was only passing through the city on her way to Mexico. She had been assigned to the MC's home in Guadalupe for the next six years.

I would not be surprised if Sister Shanta is appointed to lead the Sisters in Guadalupe. She has been an MC for over forty years and is one of those rare natural and spiritual leaders.... a gifted disciple of Jesus and of Mother Teresa.

Sister Shanta went with the Sisters one day to the park near the Golden Gate Bridge. She prayed with the homeless, the poor, the unloved, the unwanted.

Calcutta or San Francisco or Guadalupe—it doesn't matter where she is.

Like Mother Teresa ...

Sister Shanta is always working.

GENERATIONS TO COME

Sister Shanta reminded me of the novices in Calcutta and the "become-a-nurse-in-a-day" courses I taught them. "Katie, do you remember this Sister? You trained her when she was a novice." Yes, I remember her.

Sister Shanta told me that the Sister went to Nairobi—she will be in the "bush." She told Sister Shanta to tell me that she will do things the way I taught her as a nurse, especially the injections: "fast"—it causes less pain. She also told Sister to tell me that she will pass on what I had taught her and shown her.

Sister Shanta said, "You see, Katie. You have taught a generation of the Sisters. It has already been passed on. It is being passed on. And it will be passed on. All over the world."

I never thought of it that way.

I am happy. Talents and skills.

Sharing passed on ... for generations to come.

ANDY: HONORS AND A NEW CALL

Andy has a whole new path. A new door opened.

Kalighat was the preparation. Now he only has time to come on Saturdays and Sundays.

To Andy, the unloved and unwanted have always been beautiful.

Over the years as Andy served at Kalighat, he saw many come and go. Of the many who left, some came back. They had nowhere else to go, especially the young and the vulnerable, the mentally impaired. If they were left on their own, they most likely would die or starve.

Andy saw. Andy has seen it all. Life in the streets of Calcutta is brutal—you cannot win.

So God gave Andy a vision; a home for the boys. For the unwanted, the unloved, the unlovely. Andy wanted them—the more unlovely, the more Andy wanted them.

Nothing in India is simple. Red tape looms everywhere. But miracles do happen. And Andy's home became a reality. Seven boys, or perhaps more, now live in the home.

Andy's work has been noticed from afar. Mother Teresa and Sister Nirmala talked with Rome about Andy years ago.

Andy received a telephone call in India in the fall of 2004 from a Cardinal in Rome. The Cardinal called Andy on behalf of our Pope John Paul II telling him that he was invited to Rome. On November 27, 2004, the Holy Father honored Andy for his work among the poorest of the poor in Calcutta.

Andy told me, "Katie, here I was relaxing at home and the phone rings. It was this German Cardinal calling me from Rome telling me of this award. My first thought was, 'I cannot leave my children.'"

That's Andy ... humble, always thinking of others, self-less.

Andy went to Rome, meeting Pope John Paul II and the German Cardinal.

Perhaps Andy also had a small vacation.

Maybe the last rest for a long time.

SUNITA'S WEDDING

Amidst the tragedy of the tsunami, there was a very, very bright light …

The right suitor came for Sunita, and I went to the wedding!

Sunita and Lawrence got married—two hearts and two souls became one.

The date: December 30, 2004.
The place: Shishu Bhavan, Calcutta, India.
The maids of honor: two orphan friends—Shopna and Loche.
The flower girls: young friends from Shishu Bhavan.
The guests: friends from all over the world—MC Sisters, Brothers and Priests; volunteers; old, young, poor, wealthy, some famous.

It was fabulous. The story …

Sunita has a wonderful skill; she sews beautifully. Sister Sarah Grace, who now is in charge of the Shishu Bhavan, wanted her to become even more skillful, and so the MCs sent Sunita to a village about three hours from Calcutta where they have a home. In this village lives a young man named Lawrence. Lawrence also sews. Lawrence has an aging father whose body is strong, but whose mind has become weak. Lawrence cared for his father by himself. At times, Lawrence went to see the Sisters for help.

On one visit, Lawrence saw Sunita. Love at first sight. He afterwards took the train to Calcutta and asked the Sisters for permission to marry Sunita. Many men had asked for this permission in the past, but it was not given. Lawrence was different. The Sisters gave their permission, but Lawrence, as Sunita's future husband, wanted to hear her say that she also wanted this. When approached with the proposal, Sunita simply said, "I will marry." The match was made.

There is something so beautiful about a bride. Sunita was surrounded this day by a special glow; she was bathed in light. For Sunita, there was even a greater joy and happiness—someone to love and care for, and someone that would love, care for, regard, and cherish her in return—all missed in her younger years. Sunita suffered much in her younger life, yet the burn scars are a badge of beauty, reflecting the inner transformation that occurred as a result of the pain, hurt, and rejection. Sunita is a beautiful woman—inside and out.

Indian weddings are amazing, but this wedding had an "extra added bonus." All of the MC Sisters gave Sunita away—the cloistered Sisters, the active Sisters, all of them! It was a joyful Mass and ceremony. And so was the festive wedding party that followed: guests singing, Bengali drums, dancing, wonderful Indian food—all cooked by the Sisters' hands. It went on for hours and was filled with joy and happiness. God's love and blessings in abundance.

The long day was coming to a close.

Down the road to the Mother House for a visit to Mother's tomb and a final blessing. And then, it was time for the young bride and groom to go back to Lawrence's village. We rode together with the young couple to the train station through the winding, crowded streets of Calcutta—Sunita and Lawrence, now husband and wife.

Lawrence held Sunita's hand. We all walked to the train. We all smiled. We waved. We cried happy tears and said, "Good-bye!"

The train slowly pulled out. New life begins.

Another very special gift from God.

THE GERMAN CONSULATE IS BACK

The German Consulate and his wife are back in Calcutta.

I was privileged once more to be in their presence. Sister Andrea told me that they have adopted thirteen of the street children, and they are back looking after the needs of their children—education, clothing, food. I learned that one of the children they adopted is blind, another slightly retarded, another without a leg. They want to help, to love the children. Every child is special.

Spreading the fragrance.

His wife, Karin, tells me that he has been assigned to work with the United Nations, so they are twice as busy. And yet, they travel back and forth from their hectic lives in Vienna in order to spend time with their thirteen adopted children, making sure all is well. When they come, they rent a very big space so that the entire family can be together the whole time. Wow!

We visit for a few more minutes, and I watch this husband and wife walk away together, hand-in-hand. They are going to spend time with their children.

You can leave Calcutta.

But Calcutta will always be in your heart.

KATHLEEN, LEO, DOMINIC, GABRIEL, MARIA +2

Kathleen and Leo were back in China—for the third time!

Prior to adopting Maria, Kathleen and Leo had two sons of their own, Dominic and Gabriel. After adopting Maria, Kathleen and Leo again went to China and adopted another daughter.

They brought home Teresa. Kathleen and Leo named her after Mother.

In June of 2005, they were back in China again. They adopted Isaac, their fifth child.

Mother Teresa may not have established a home in China, but her robe is doing wonders.

JEREMIAH—LESSONS LEARNED

India was not done with Jeremiah. Nor was Jeremiah done with India.

India and Calcutta are lessons in life. Once you have been there, even if you do not return, you will never forget your lesson. It's a process that speeds up the development of your heart and soul.

Upon returning home from Calcutta, Jeremiah couldn't adjust. He missed the brutality, the intensity of Calcutta.

As extreme as Calcutta and India are, they are also very beautiful. When you leave your home in the West, you leave behind familiarity. When you arrive in India, you are set down in the midst of unreality … chaos, noise, pollution, disease, all the unlovely things. Right away you long for the mundane—things at home like a simple trip to the store, milk and bread, anything but "this." Then when you return home, you long for India and all that goes with it.

Jeremiah packed his bags and returned. He went back to work, caring for the poor of Calcutta. He was there again for months.

Jeremiah wrote me once again from Calcutta. He was on his way home. He wasn't sure what he would do next. Maybe work on an organic farm, do some fishing. He has to sort all this out.

Life's lessons are being learned well.

India is life-changing.

Jeremiah's journey is continuing.

THE FACE OF MEDICINE

After Calcutta, my daughter, Linda, was never the same. She never looked back.

When we came home that year, Linda said, "Mom, I'm going to be a doctor. And maybe I'll do research on malaria or maybe just go back to India and work for a while."

On May 22, 2005, Linda graduated from Georgetown University's Medical School. We were all there—my mother and my three sisters, Nick and Julie with my grandson Derek, Gig with my granddaughter Autumn, and me. We were all beaming.

All of the one hundred and fifty new doctors had accomplished a tremendous goal. To be a doctor is truly to be God's hands in a very needy world. The Assistant Surgeon General, Dr. Kevin Kiley, gave the commencement address. He made all of us proud to be American.

Awards were bestowed. Many of the new doctors were honored, and Linda received the award for highest achievement in her chosen residency of Internal Medicine.

Dr. Donald Knowland is 87 years old and teaches at the University. He was Linda's mentor. He told me that Linda was his "all-time favorite student." We talked about the sad state of medicine today, with so many people falling through the cracks or who can't afford help.

Dr. Knowland agreed. And then he said, "Linda will change the face of medicine."

I know that and I'm very proud.

THE SAINTS

I suspect that Pope John Paul II and Mother Teresa are having some pretty interesting conversations.

An eternity to share their experiences ... of God and his love.

978-0-595-70783-0
0-595-70783-1

Printed in the United States
103683LV00002B/13-21/P